EUROPE AFTER THE COLD WAR

An Instructional Guide for High Schools

By Joyce Kaufman, Mary Teague Mason, Daniel S. Papp, D. William Tinkler, and Julia J. White

To be used in conjunction with the Southern Center for International Studies' Six-Part Videotape, "Europe After the Cold War," featuring excerpts from the Southern Center's Dean Rusk Interviews, Annual Meetings of the Former U.S. Secretaries of State and Defense, and Annual Meetings of Former World Leaders.

Published by

The Southern Center for International Studies
Atlanta, Georgia
1994

Supported by a grant from the
JOSEPH B. WHITEHEAD FOUNDATION

SPONSORS

The Southern Center for International Studies wishes to thank the Joseph B.Whitehead Foundation for its funding of this educational package. We also wish to thank the following contributors for their assistance in the production of the videotapes:

Arkansas' Excelsior Hotel
Arkansas Power and Light Company
  and Energy Corporation
BellSouth
BellSouth International
Berlin Hilton
Berliner Zeitung
BMW-Niederlassung Berlin
George V. Brown
Canon Virginia, Incorporated
Coordination Council for North American
  Affairs
Eagle Forensic Laboratory
Exxon Education Foundation
Ford Foundation
John & Mary Franklin Foundation
Fulbright Institute of International
  Relations
J. B. Fuqua
General Dynamics
Grumman Corporation
Walter S. Huff, Jr. Foundation

The Landmarks Group
LBJ Foundation
Lockheed Aeronautical Systems
Loridans Foundation
Lufthansa German Airlines
Newport News Shipbuilding
Norfolk Southern Corporation
State of Alabama
State of Arkansas
State of Georgia
State of Maine
Stephen's Incorporated
Trust Company Bank
J. M. Tull Foundation
Union Camp
University of Georgia
University of Georgia Foundation
Volvo
The Willet Fund
Wooley Foundation
Worthen Banking Corporation

1994 The Southern Center for International Studies
    All Rights Reserved

International Standard Book Number: 0-935082-18-2

This publication is made available through a grant from the Joseph B. Whitehead Foundation.

Requests for copies should be addressed to:

The Southern Center for International Studies
320 West Paces Ferry Road, N.W.
Atlanta, Georgia 30305

NOTICE OF NONDISCRIMINATION POLICY AS TO STUDENTS

The Southern Center for International Studies admits students of any race, color, handicap, age, sex, sexual orientation, marital status, religion, national and ethnic origin to all the rights, privileges, programs and activities generally accorded or made available to students of the Center. It does not discriminate on the basis of race, color, handicap, age, sex, sexual orientation, marital status, religion, national and ethnic origin in administration of its educational policies, admissions policies, scholarship and loan programs, and other center-administered programs.

PREFACE

In 1991, recognizing that the world was experiencing incredibly rapid and important changes, the Southern Center for International Studies (SCIS) began a major project to develop educational packages for secondary schools and universities based on the annual SCIS meetings of former U.S. Secretaries of State and Defense, and the SCIS conferences of Former World Leaders.

The purpose of the project and the educational packages that it develops is straightforward: to provide for educators and their students up-to-date information, analysis, and lessons about contemporary international issues and events that go beyond resource materials that are available in most textbooks.

Although SCIS constructs its educational packages to emphasize contemporary international issues and events, SCIS also recognizes the importance of history and culture in understanding contemporary international affairs. However, historical and cultural materials are widely available in resources already available to educators. Therefore, SCIS consciously placed its emphasis on contemporary issues and events as it developed its educational packages.

The Southern Center published its first educational packages in this project, <u>The End of the Soviet Union</u>, in 1992. It has received widespread critical acclaim. Already in use in over 500 classrooms in six states, <u>The End of the Soviet Union</u> has been selected by the College Board for inclusion on its list of recommended materials for Advanced Placement courses.

The present publication, <u>Europe After the Cold War</u>, is the second educational package in this project. Like <u>The End of the Soviet Union</u>, <u>Europe After the Cold War</u> contains four core elements: 1.) videotaped excerpts from the Southern Center's Dean Rusk tapes, and from meetings of the former U.S. Secretaries of State, the former U.S. Secretaries of Defense, and the former World Leaders, in which these prominent former officials discuss issues and events related to the educational package; 2.) transcripts of the videotapes; 3.) a study guide that provides critical background information needed to understand the issues and events under discussion; and 4.) a set of lessons which enables teachers to provide a rich and diversified educational experience for their classes.

SCIS educational packages offer teachers four significant advantages. The first advantage is <u>quality</u>. They have been assembled by outstanding scholars and teachers, and are well-organized and concise. They offer an easily-available wealth of information and analysis that teachers need.

Second, they provide <u>context</u>. Current issues and events are set in a broader background than that in which they ordinarily appear. Thus, they have greater meaning for students.

Third, they are <u>comprehensive</u>. The packages examine current issues and events from different perspectives, and they use a multi-media approach designed to hold students' attention. Thus, they enhance understanding.

Fourth, they are <u>current</u>. Because of the Southern Center's rapid pen-to-press production, the packages are up-to-date. What is more, beginning in 1994, SCIS will update each package annually as issues and events warrant, based on the yearly meetings of the Secretaries and the former World Leaders.

Southern Center instructional packages are quite flexible, and are designed so that teachers have several options about how to use them. Given the thematic construction of the package, any one of the individual parts of each package may be used as each teacher believes appropriate for her or his class. As a second option, since each part of every educational package includes several separate classroom activities, teachers may choose to use only one or two classroom activities from each part of an educational package. A third option is to use an entire educational package, thereby providing students with an excellent in-depth understanding of the region or issue-area that is being studied. Regardless of which option is chosen, students will develop a much fuller understanding of contemporary international affairs and the forces that drive them than they have ever had before.

Given the rapidity of change in today's world, and the difficulty we all have in keeping up with it, the Southern Center believes its educational packages provide teachers and students alike an important tool to keep abreast of international issues and events, and to understand what those issues and events mean for them.

TABLE OF CONTENTS

ABOUT THE AUTHORS

KAUFMAN, Joyce. Co-author of the Study Guide. Professor of Political Science at Whittier College. Author of several books and articles on European political, economic, and security affairs. Former Visiting Professor at the University of Maryland. B.A., New York University. Ph.D., University of Maryland.

MASON, Mary Teague. Co-author of the Lesson Plans. Teacher at Dacula (Georgia) High School, and a social studies consultant, K-12. Teacher of the Year, Gwinnett county (Georgia) 1987-88. State of Georgia Social Studies Award, 1992. B.S., Huntingdon College. M.Ed., Auburn University at Montgomery. Specialist Degree, Emory University.

PAPP, Daniel S. Co-author of the Study Guide and Project Co-Director. Professor of International Affairs at the Georgia Institute of Technology. Author of seven books and over 60 articles on a variety of issues in U.S. foreign and defense policy. Southern Center Educational Projects Director. B.A., Dartmouth College. Ph.D., University of Miami (Coral Gables).

TINKLER, D. William. Co-author of the Lesson Plans. Administrator at Taylor Road Middle School (Fulton County, Georgia). Former Coordinator of Secondary Level Social Studies for Fulton County. Consultant on Social Studies Education. B.A., Duke University. M.Ed. and Ed.D., University of Georgia.

WHITE, Julia Johnson. Videotape Producer and Project Co-Director. Vice President, Legal Counsel, and Co-Founder of the Southern Center for International Studies. Executive Producer and Producer of the Southern Center's Peabody Award-winning television programs on the Conferences of the Former U.S. Secretaries of State, Defense, and the Treasury. M.B.A., Emory University. J.D., Emory School of Law.

BIOGRAPHICAL SKETCHES OF THE
FORMER U.S. SECRETARIES OF STATE

BAKER, James. Secretary of State from 1989 to 1992 under President Bush. Directed Presidential Election Campaigns for Presidents Ford, Reagan, and Bush. White House Chief of Staff under President Reagan, 1981 to 1985. Secretary of the Treasury, 1985 to 1988. White House Chief of Staff under President Bush, 1992-1993.

Mr. Baker was Secretary of State during the Eastern European revolutions of 1989, the unification of Germany, the beginning efforts of Eastern European states to construct post-communist societies, the first stages of the implementation of the Single European Act, the collapse of the Soviet Union, the Persian Gulf War, and the beginning of the U.S. reappraisal of its role in post-Cold War Europe.

EAGLEBURGER, Lawrence. Secretary of State from 1992 to 1993 under President Bush. Entered the U.S. Foreign Service in 1957. Ambassador to Yugoslavia, 1977-1981. Assistant Secretary of State for European Affairs, 1981-1982. Undersecretary of State for Political Affairs, 1982-1989. Deputy Secretary of State from 1989 to 1992.

Mr. Eagleburger was Secretary of State as Eastern European states struggled to construct post-communist societies, as the U.S. reassessed its post-Cold War role in Europe, and as Western Europe moved toward greater political and economic integration under the Single European Act and the Maastricht Treaty.

HAIG, Alexander. Secretary of State from 1981 to 1982 under President Reagan. Deputy Assistant to the President for National Security Affairs, 1970 to 1973 under President Nixon, and White House Chief of Staff, 1973 to 1975 under President Ford. Served as Supreme Allied Commander in Europe from 1975 until 1979.

Mr. Haig was Secretary of State during the heightened U.S.-Soviet tensions of the first Reagan administration and the accompanying U.S. military build-up, the declaration of martial law in Poland, the Falklands/Malvinas War, and rising tensions in Europe over the scheduled 1983 deployment of intermediate nuclear forces.

KISSINGER, Henry. Secretary of State from 1973 to 1977 under Presidents Nixon and Ford. Assistant to the President for National Security Affairs from 1969 to 1975 under Presidents Nixon and Ford. Awarded the Nobel Peace Prize in 1973 for his efforts in arranging a cease-fire in Vietnam.

Mr. Kissinger was Secretary of State during the Helsinki Conference on Security and Cooperation in Europe, the beginning of the Mutual and Balanced Force Reduction talks, and the general improvement in East-West relations that took place in Europe during the Ford administration.

MUSKIE, Edmund. Secretary of State from 1980 to 1981 under President Carter. Governor of Maine from 1954 to 1958, and U.S. Senator from Maine, 1958 to 1980. In 1968, he was the Democratic Party's nominee for Vice President. Since his tenure as Secretary of State, he has been senior partner in a law firm.

Mr. Muskie was Secretary of State during the development of the Solidarity trade union movement in Poland, the deterioration in U.S.-Soviet relations caused by the Soviet invasion of Afghanistan, and the acceleration of U.S. concern over Soviet activities elsewhere in the Developing World.

ROGERS, William. Secretary of State from 1969 to 1973 under President Nixon. Attorney General from 1957 to 1961 under President Eisenhower and U.S. Representative to the Twentieth Session of the U.N. General Assembly. In 1986, he was the Chairperson on the Presidential Commission on the Challenger Disaster.

Mr. Rogers was Secretary of State during the Nixon-Brezhnev detente, the beginning of West Germany's policy of "Ostpolitik," the 1972 Four Power Accord on the status of Berlin, and the 1972 East German-West German accord on mutual recognition.

RUSK, Dean. Secretary of State from 1961 to 1969 under Presidents Kennedy and Johnson. Assistant Secretary of State for United Nations Affairs and for Far Eastern Affairs, 1947 to 1952. From 1952 until 1960, he was President of the Rockefeller Foundation. Since 1970, he has been a professor at the University of Georgia.

Mr. Rusk was Secretary of State during the Bay of Pigs invasion, the Cuban Missile Crisis, the U.S.-Soviet detente following that crisis, and the Soviet invasion of Czechoslovakia. He was Secretary of State during the early years of the Vietnam War.

SHULTZ, George. Secretary of State from 1982 to 1989 under President Reagan. From 1946 to 1957, he was a faculty member at M.I.T., and from 1962 to 1968, he was a Dean at the University of Chicago. He was U.S. Secretary of Labor from 1969 to 1970, and Secretary of the Treasury and Assistant to President Nixon, 1972 to 1974.

Mr. Schultz was Secretary of State during the improvement in East-West relations that accompanied the Gorbachev reforms in Europe, the many Reagan-Gorbachev summit meetings of 1985-1989, the conclusion of the Single European Act, and a series of minor and major disagreements between the U.S. and its European allies about how to respond to the changes taking place in Eastern Europe and the Soviet Union.

VANCE, Cyrus. Secretary of State from 1977 to 1980 under President Carter. In 1961, he was appointed General Counsel to the Department of Defense. He was appointed Secretary of the Army in 1962 and Deputy Secretary of Defense in 1964, and served as U.N. Special Envoy to Yugoslavia, 1991 to 1992.

Mr. Vance was Secretary of State when the Soviet Union invaded Afghanistan, as the Solidarity trade union movement in Poland first developed, and as the remaining vestiges of the East-West detente of the 1970s ended.

BIOGRAPHICAL SKETCHES OF THE
FORMER U.S. SECRETARIES OF DEFENSE

BROWN, Harold. Secretary of Defense from 1977 to 1981 under President Carter. Other posts he has held include Director of the Lawrence Livermore Laboratory, Secretary of the Air Force, Undersecretary of Defense, President of the California Institute of Technology, and a member of the U.S. delegation to the Strategic Arms Limitation Talks.

Mr. Brown was Secretary of Defense when the Soviet Union invaded Afghanistan, as the Solidarity trade union movement in Poland first developed, as the East-West detente of the 1970s ended, and as the U.S. began its defense build-up under President Carter.

CARLUCCI, Frank. Secretary of Defense from 1987 to 1989 under President Reagan. Prior to that time he served as Assistant to the President for National Security Affairs. He has also been Deputy Director of Central Intelligence, President and Chief Operating Officer of Sears World Trade, and U.S. Ambassador to Portugal.

Mr. Carlucci was Secretary of Defense when more and more people in the West began to realize that the Gorbachev reforms were significantly reducing the Soviet threat, when the Intermediate Nuclear Forces Treaty was signed, and as NATO began rethinking its mission as a result both of changes in the U.S.S.R. and increased European integration.

CHENEY, Richard. Secretary of Defense from 1989 to 1993 under President Bush. He served as Assistant to the President and White House Chief of Staff under the Ford administration. He also has been a six term U.S. Congressman from Wyoming.

Mr. Cheney was Secretary of Defense during the defense draw-down that followed the collapse of communism in Eastern Europe and the Soviet Union, during Operations Desert Storm and Desert Shield, and during the efforts to redefine NATO's mission following the dissolution of the U.S.S.R.

CLIFFORD, Clark. Secretary of Defense from 1968 to 1969 under President Johnson. He also was Special Counsel to President Truman, and a member of the President's Foreign Intelligence Advisory Board.

Mr. Clifford was Secretary of Defense when the decision was made not to send more U.S. troops to Vietnam, and when the Soviet Union invaded Czechoslovakia.

LAIRD, Melvin. Secretary of Defense from 1969 to 1973 under President Nixon. He was elected to the 83rd Congress in 1952 and served in that capacity for the next eight terms. In 1973, he was named Counselor to the President for Domestic Affairs.

Mr. Laird was Secretary of Defense during the final U.S. withdrawal from Vietnam, the development of the Brezhnev-Nixon detente, the signing of the SALT I and ABM Treaties, the development of cordial U.S.-Chinese relations, and the decline in tensions in Europe that marked the early 1970s.

McNAMARA, Robert. Secretary of Defense from 1961 to 1968 under Presidents Kennedy and Johnson. He was named President of the Ford Motor Company in 1960, and was President of the World Bank from 1968 to 1981.

Mr. McNamara was Secretary of Defense during the Bay of Pigs and the Cuban Missile Crisis, the U.S. military build-up in Vietnam and the height of the Vietnam War, the signing of the Nuclear Test Ban Treaty, and during the negotiations that led to the signing of the Nuclear Non-Proliferation Treaty.

RICHARDSON, Elliot. Secretary of Defense in 1973 under President Nixon. Other posts he has held include U.S. Ambassador to Great Britain, Secretary of Commerce, Attorney General, Special U.S. Representative to the Law of the Seas Conference, and Undersecretary of State.

Mr. Richardson was Secretary of Defense during the last year of the Nixon presidency as the United States ended its involvement in the Vietnam War.

RUMSFELD, Donald. Secretary of Defense from 1975 to 1977 under President Ford. He also served as White House Chief of Staff under President Ford, U.S. Ambassador to NATO, President Reagan's Special Middle Eastern Envoy, and Chief Executive Officer of Searle Pharmaceutical Company.

Mr. Rumsfeld was Secretary of Defense during the period of cordial East-West relations in Europe that followed the Helsinki Conference on Security and Cooperation in Europe, and during the Soviet-supported Cuban build-up in Angola.

SCHLESINGER, James. Secretary of Defense from 1973 to 1975 under Presidents Nixon and Ford. He has also been Acting Director of the Office of Management and the Budget, Chairman of the Atomic Energy Agency, Director of the CIA, and Secretary of Energy.

Mr. Schlesinger was Secretary of Defense during the Ford-Brezhnev Summit in Vladivostok, and during the continued improvement in East-West relations in Europe that took place before the Helsinki Conference on Security and Cooperation in Europe.

WEINBERGER, Caspar. Secretary of Defense from 1981 to 1987 under President Reagan. He has also been Chairman of the Federal Trade Commission, Director of the Office of Management and Budget, and Secretary of Health, Education and Welfare.

Mr. Weinberger was Secretary of Defense when the Reagan administration instituted its large U.S. military build-up, during the period of heightened U.S.-Soviet tensions during the early and middle 1980s, as the U.S. began its active opposition to pro-Soviet states in the Third World, and when U.S.-Soviet relations improved during the late 1980s.

BIOGRAPHICAL SKETCHES OF
WORLD LEADERS

CALLAGHAN, James. Served as Prime Minister of the United Kingdom from 1976 to 1979. He has also been Chancellor of the Exchequer, Home Secretary, Prime Minister and First Lord of the Treasury. In 1987, James Callaghan was created Knight of the Garter and made a Life Peer, becoming Lord Callaghan of Cardiff KG. He is President of Swansea University College, University of Wales.

NAKASONE, Yasuhiro. Served as Prime Minister of Japan from 1982 to 1987. He held the cabinet posts of Minister of State and Director of Science and Technology, Minister of State, Director of General Defense, and Minister of International Trade and Industry. He has also served in Japan's House of Representatives, and is the Chairman of the International Institute for Global Peace (IIGP).

SCHMIDT, Helmut. Served as Chancellor of the Federal Republic of Germany from 1974 to 1982. Before becoming the fifth Chancellor of the Federal Republic of Germany, he was a member of the Social Democratic municipal government of Hamburg. In 1953, he was elected to the Bundestag in Bonn, where he later served as Secretary of Defense and Secretary of Economics and Finance. Dr. Schmidt has also been publisher of *Die Zeit*.

BIOGRAPHICAL SKETCHES OF MODERATORS

GERGEN, David. Mr. Gergen was appointed Counselor to the President by President Clinton in 1993. Earlier in his career, he served eight years in the White House under three other presidents, Nixon, Ford and Reagan. He has also been an editor-at-large with U.S. News & World Report, during which time he also was a commentator on television and radio.

KALB, Marvin. Marvin Kalb is the Edward R. Murrow Professor of Press and Public Safety Policy at Harvard University's John F. Kennedy School of Government, and Director of the Joan Shorenstein Barone Center on the Press, Politics and Public Policy. He has also served as diplomatic correspondent and anchorman at CBS and NBC, and moderator of Meet the Press.

NEWMAN, Edwin. For 31 years before his retirement, Mr. Newman was a correspondent , anchorman, and essayist for NBC. He has received the Overseas Press Club Award, numerous Emmys, and other awards for journalism from the Universities of Wisconsin and Ohio. Mr. Newman is also the author of several books.

SMITH, Hedrick. Mr. Smith is the former New York Times Moscow Bureau Chief, and a frequent commentator on U.S. television on current domestic U.S. and international political, economic, and social affairs. He is the author of The Russians and The New Russians, as well as several other books.

ACKNOWLEDGEMENTS

These teaching packages have been made possible through the untiring efforts of many individuals working collectively in order to achieve the highest degree of excellence possible in the production of these materials.

Our first acknowledgement goes to the Joseph B. Whitehead Foundation for funding this project. Without the Whitehead Foundation, none of this would have been possible.

I wish to thank Tom Johnson and Kathy Christensen of CNN, the MacNeil Lehrer Hour, and ARD Network, Germany for allowing us to use news footage for the videotape and Peter White III and his colleagues, Elizabeth Callan, Patricia Ellis, Frank Fitzmaurice and Karen Watson for making the videotapes more student-friendly and interesting by incorporating this footage into excerpts from conferences with the Secretaries. Additionally, I would like to thank Crawford Post Productions for assisting in this project.

I also wish to thank Felicia Moore for assisting in the editing of the conference videotapes; Dale Tyree for his critique and editing of the instructional manual; Marcia Hoinville, Kelli Fisher, Cassady Craft and Tom Scollard for their assistance in researching the Center's conference tapes and transcripts for needed subject matter; Linda Helms for her independent evaluation of the educational materials; Richard Gentry and Vance Mason for their technical assistance on finalizing the instructional manual; Gloria Pope for her administrative support; and Diane Sloan for assisting the authors and producers in coordinating the project and for preparing the transcripts.

A special thank you is offered to Dr. Werner Rogers, Georgia's State Superintendent of Schools, to Dr. James Fox, Superintendent of Fulton County Schools, and to the Center's Educational Advisory Council members who offered valuable insight and advice before and during the preparation of these materials. Council members assisting in this project were: Gwen Hutcheson, Greg Duncan, Glen Blankenship, Louisa Moffitt, Marcia Humbert, Carole Hahn, Ben Crosby, Ann Goellner and Karen Lowe.

There are two other individuals whose contributions have been felt in many ways: Peter White, who is most responsible for making this project possible; and Dr. Cedric Suzman, who gave advice and council every step of the way.

Julia Johnson White
Vice President and
Producer

INTRODUCTION

The late 1980s and early 1990s have been times of immense change for Europe. In 1989, Eastern Europeans overthrew the communist governments that had ruled them for almost half a century. The following year, Germany, divided since World War II, united. In 1991, the Soviet Union broke up, ending the military threat that had haunted Western Europe since World War II.

Also in 1991, the leaders of the twelve European Community states concluded the Maastricht Treaty, which if implemented would lead to the creation of a United States of Europe in everything but name. Meanwhile, Eastern Europeans expressed concern that Western Europe was guarding its economic prosperity, keeping Eastern Europe at arm's length.

As these events occurred, ethnic tension and hatred swept many states. In Yugoslavia, ethnic strife exploded into civil war, and thousands were killed. Ethnic nationalism also led Czechs and Slovaks to engineer a peaceful dissolution of Czechoslovakia. Simultaneously, anti-foreign sentiment swelled in France, Germany, and elsewhere as well, leading to fears that neo-Nazism was on the rise.

Amid this ferment, the world's two erstwhile superpowers, the United States and Russia, wondered what roles remained for them in Europe. For nearly fifty years, the U.S. and the Soviet Union confronted each other over Europe. By the mid-1990s, neither Washington nor Moscow clearly understood what its role in Europe might be.

What, then, is the future of post-Cold War Europe? Will Europe move toward greater and greater integration, possibly even unification? Or will European countries and peoples resume their long history of internal fighting that twice this century led to world war? How will European events and issues affect the United States?

These are difficult questions to answer. In this Southern Center for International Studies educational package, we will first, in a background lesson, explore the role that Europe played in the Cold War. We will then examine five important current sets of European issues: 1.) the fall of Eastern European communism; 2.) the European Union; 3.) nationalism in Europe; 4.) the German question; and 5.) European security.

BACKGROUND LESSON

THE COLD WAR IN EUROPE

Background Lesson of 6 Lesson Plans for the
Southern Center for International Studies'
High School Educational Package
EUROPE AFTER THE COLD WAR

The leaders of the "Big Three" World War II allies -Prime Minister Winston Churchill of Great Britain, President Franklin Roosevelt of the United States, and General Secretary Joseph Stalin of the Soviet Union- met at Yalta in February 1945 to try to agree on how the post-World War II world should be shaped.

Study Guide for

**BACKGROUND LESSON
of the SCIS Educational Package**
EUROPE AFTER THE COLD WAR

**THE COLD WAR
IN EUROPE**

World War II took a fearful toll on Europe. No completely accurate accounting of the costs of the conflict are possible, but when the European phase of the war ended in May 1945, over 40 million Europeans had been killed. Virtually every economy in Europe had been ravaged by the war and was at a standstill. Throughout Europe, governments and societies had to be reconstructed from scratch. In all recorded history, no war had ever been as destructive.

But who would reconstruct Europe, and what model would be used? That was the central question that faced the victorious Allies at the end of the war, the so-called "Big Three" of Great Britain, the Soviet Union, and the United States. Each had its own view of what post-World War II Europe should be like.

Great Britain and the United States had similar views. Both preferred European states with democratic governments and free market economies, and both wanted Germany to be economically prosperous but not militaristic. From the U.S. and British perspectives, this would prevent Germany from seeking revenge for its defeats in World Wars I and II.

The Soviet view was different. The U.S.S.R. wanted pro-Soviet, preferably communist, governments with centralized economic and political decision-making systems in Europe. Also, the U.S.S.R. wanted to punish Germany for the destruction it inflicted on the Soviet Union during World War II, and to make sure that Germany could never again initiate a major war. The U.S.S.R. therefore wanted post-World War II Germany to be weak.

All three victorious countries recognized that despite the devastation it had suffered, Europe, with its highly educated and skilled population, remained an extremely important player in world affairs. Indeed, in many respects, the Cold War that dominated international affairs from the late 1940s to the late 1980s began because of East-West disagreement over the future of Europe.

The Slide Toward the Cold War: 1945-1947

As the European phase of World War II ended in May 1945, hopes ran high that the victors could construct a peaceful and stable post-World War II international system. However, the Big Three were divided by mistrust over how World War II was conducted, held different views of how post-World War II Europe should be structured, and were wedded to opposed ideological outlooks. Thus, the Cold War slowly developed.

The confrontation was called the Cold War for a basic reason: the two sides, one led by the United States and the other by the Soviet Union, opposed each other, but no military conflict took place.

The two sides disagreed about many issues, but the two most important were the future of Eastern Europe and the future of Germany. Even before World War II was over, it was evident that these two issues would become extremely important after the war. When the leaders of the Big Three met at Teheran, Iran in late 1943, Yalta, U.S.S.R. in early 1945, and Potsdam, Germany in mid-1945, these questions were central agenda items. Despite detailed records of these conferences, disagreement exists even today about what actually was decided at these conferences about the future of Eastern Europe and the future of Germany.

However, there is no debate about what actually happened. Germany was divided into four occupation zones, one each for the Big Three and a fourth for France. Germany's capital, Berlin, located deep within the Soviet zone of occupation, was also divided into four zones for the four occupying countries. France, Great Britain, and the United States each were guaranteed access to Berlin by one road and by one air corridor apiece.

Here, it is important to address the role of France in post-World War II Europe. Long one of the major powers in Europe, France had been overrun by Nazi Germany in 1940. Thus, it was not part of the Big Three. Nevertheless, Free French forces under General Charles de Gaulle played an active role in the war against Germany. Given France's long-standing importance in Europe and the role that the Free French played in the war against Germany, France therefore was once again viewed as a major power after World War II ended.

Meanwhile, in Eastern Europe, the Soviet Union, often with the help of local communists, set up pro-Soviet regimes in Bulgaria, Hungary, Poland, and Romania as the Soviet Army advanced westward during 1945. By 1947, these regimes had become communist. The Soviet Army remained encamped in these countries. In Albania and Yugoslavia, local communist leaders set up their own communist governments. At the same time, multiparty democratic governments came to power in Western Europe and Czechoslovakia.

Throughout these years (1945-47), the United States retained significant influence in Western Europe. Nevertheless, by 1947, the U.S. had withdrawn virtually all of its armed forces from Europe. Once again, as after World War I, the United States flirted with isolationism.

But the U.S. had not abandoned all of its foreign interests. It retained a vital interest in Europe's future, and complained earnestly to the Soviets about the U.S.S.R.'s efforts to promote communism in Eastern Europe and its zone of occupation in Germany. U.S.-Soviet relations also deteriorated in early 1946 because of events in Turkey and Iran. In Turkey, the Soviet Union pressured the Turkish government to give it access to the straits that connect the Black Sea and the Mediterranean Sea. Backed by the U.S., which sent warships to Turkey to show support, Turkey rejected the Russian demand. Also in early 1946, the U.S.S.R. refused to withdraw its forces from northern Iran until the United States sent a sternly-worded message to Moscow.

The Cold War Begins: 1947-1954

It cannot be said with certainty when the Cold War began. U.S.-Soviet tension escalated between 1945 and 1947 because of disagreements over Eastern Europe, Germany, Iran, and Turkey, and because each side feared that the other would launch a military attack. To the United States and its Allies, the Soviet Army was poised to invade Western Europe, vulnerable because of the American military withdrawal from the continent. To the Soviet Union, the American military withdrawal from Europe meant little because the United States was the only country with nuclear weapons. Further, after the U.S. dropped atomic bombs on Hiroshima and Nagasaki in Japan to end World War II in the Pacific in 1945, the U.S.S.R. recognized that the U.S. was willing to use such weapons. Meanwhile, in Greece, a civil war between the royalist government and insurgent communists raged. Great Britain supported the government, providing military and economic assistance. The communist insurgents received outside aid from Yugoslavia and other communist states. Concentrating on larger European problems, the United States had little interest in the Greek civil war, considering it to be Great Britain's problem.

This changed on February 21, 1947, when Great Britain informed the U.S. that because of its own war-weakened economy, it could no longer provide assistance to either Greece or Turkey. At the end of March, London informed Washington, Great Britain intended to withdraw from Greece.

U.S. President Harry Truman faced a dilemma. If Great Britain stopped supporting Greece, then communist insurgents would probably emerge victorious there. If that happened, then Turkey would be isolated and vulnerable to Soviet pressure. The only way to prevent this, Truman believed, was for the United States to replace Great Britain in support of the government in Greece.

After considerable debate within the U.S. government, Truman acted. On March 12, 1947, Truman delivered a speech to a joint session of Congress in which he declared that "it must be the policy of the United States to support free peoples who are resisting attempted subjugation by armed minorities or by outside pressures." The Truman Doctrine had been born.

The Truman Doctrine was important for several reasons. First, it provided aid to Greece and Turkey. Second, it committed the United States to oppose communist and other expansion in Europe and elsewhere. Third, it for all practical purposes ended the post-World War II debate in the United States about whether the U.S. should return to isolationism. Fourth, it ended the almost two-century-old U.S. tradition of remaining aloof from European affairs except in wartime.

The Truman Doctrine was only the first step in the United States' new resolve to play a larger role in Europe. Recognizing that the economy of virtually every European state was in shambles, understanding that without a massive infusion of economic assistance there was almost no hope of economic recovery, and fearing that Western Europe's sorry economic condition was fertile ground for communist expansion, U.S. Secretary of State George Marshall, on June 5, 1947, called on European states to draw up a continent-wide plan for economic assistance to be provided by the United States. The Marshall Plan, later described by British Prime Minister Winston Churchill as the most generous act in humankind's history, had been conceived.

In response to the U.S. idea, in late August 1947, 16 Western European states submitted a request to the United States for $28 billion in aid. In December 1947, Truman presented the request, reduced to $17 billion, to Congress. But Congress, concerned about the cost of the program, the possibility of socialism in Europe, and the danger of nationalization of U.S. property there, refused to act.

Then came the communist coup in Czechoslovakia. After World War II, U.S. and Soviet troops withdrew from Czechoslovakia as the two had agreed. A constitutional democracy was established and appeared to be functioning reasonably well despite tension between non-communists and communists. Then, in February 1948, the communists engineered a successful coup, and Czechoslovakia became communist. The following month, the U.S. Congress approved the Marshall Plan. Europe was now clearly divided into East and West.

Soon after, East-West tensions escalated still further as the Soviet Union, in June 1948, blocked all land routes into Berlin. The Berlin Blockade, instituted by the Kremlin because it objected to the unification of the U.S., British, and French occupation zones into a single West Germany, went on for eleven months. For the entire period, the Western Allies supplied Berlin by air as East-West tensions rose.

The coup in Czechoslovakia and the Berlin Blockade convinced many in Western Europe and the United States that concrete security links were needed between North America and Western Europe. Thus, after extensive negotiation, Belgium, Canada, Denmark, France, Great Britain, Iceland, Italy, Luxembourg, the Netherlands, Norway, Portugal, and the United States, in April 1949, signed the North Atlantic Treaty. Under the Treaty, the twelve signatory countries pledged to defend each other should any be attacked. The North Atlantic Treaty also served as the basis for the creation of the North Atlantic Treaty Organization (NATO). With the creation of NATO, U.S., Canadian and Western European security was now tightly coupled. In addition, NATO politically linked the U.S. with Western Europe through a formal alliance.

Although created in 1949, NATO did not become militarily meaningful until 1950. The impetus for NATO to become a meaningful military alliance was the June 1950 North Korean invasion of South Korea. To Western European and North American leaders, the invasion of South Korea made it appear as if the Soviet Union and its allies, newly strengthened by the Soviet acquisition of nuclear weapons in 1949 and the victory of communism in China the same year, intended to launch a global campaign of military aggression. These fears led the U.S. to deploy U.S. troops, aircraft, and nuclear weapons to Western Europe in the early 1950s under NATO auspices.

Despite this military buildup, U.S. and Western European leaders remained concerned that Europe was not secure. By the early 1950s, Europe, growing stronger as the result of Marshall Plan aid and Western European hard work, was even more of a prize than it had been at the end of World War II. Perceiving the Soviet threat to be growing, Western European and North American leaders believed that Western Europe's defense had to be strengthened still more. The question was, "How?"

One answer was West German rearmament. However, this raised concerns in many countries on both sides of the Iron Curtain. One proposal was to create a European Defense Community (EDC) that included West Germany. However, this proposal was defeated by the French National Assembly in August 1954. Two months later, West Germany was invited to join NATO, which it did in 1955. In response, the Soviet Union created the Warsaw Treaty Organization, or Warsaw Pact, which included Bulgaria, Czechoslovakia, East Germany, Hungary, Poland, Rumania, and the U.S.S.R.

Coexistence and Confrontation Part I: 1955-1962

Even as West Germany joined NATO and the Soviets created the Warsaw Pact, other events moderated East-West tensions. The Austrian State Treaty and the Geneva Summit were the most notable.

On May 15, 1955, the U.S. and the Soviet Union signed the Austrian State Treaty, under which all foreign forces withdrew from Austria and Austria received its independence as a permanently neutral state. Two months later, U.S. President Dwight Eisenhower and Soviet Premier Nikita Khrushchev met in Geneva in the first U.S.-Soviet summit meeting since the end of World War II.

The Geneva summit did not produce any concrete results, but nevertheless, a new friendly "Spirit of Geneva" permeated European affairs and East-West relations. Unfortunately, this did not last. Trouble had been brewing in the Soviet Union's Eastern European empire for some time, and in 1956 it erupted.

In Poland, workers took to the streets in opposition to price increases, working conditions, and the communist government. Surprisingly, the Polish Communist Party acknowledged the legitimacy of some of the complaints. It changed leaders and adopted several policy directions at odds with those of the U.S.S.R. Poles responded favorably to their government's new directions. Poland was still communist, but it had established a degree of its own policy direction.

Hungary fared less well. In Hungary, a popular uprising in October 1956 led to the creation of a new government that appeared likely to eliminate communist rule and withdraw Hungary from the Warsaw Pact. The Soviet Union sent in its armed forces and crushed the Hungarian revolution. Hundreds were killed, and thousands fled to the West. East-West relations plunged into a Cold War freeze.

The Cold War continued during 1957 and most of 1958 without any significant European-related crises. Then, in November 1958, Khrushchev demanded that the West withdraw its forces from Berlin, declared all previous agreements on Berlin null and void, and threatened to sign a peace treaty with East Germany and turn all access routes to Berlin over to East Germany unless Soviet demands were met within six months. Berlin was again a flashpoint that threatened to escalate into general war.

Despite the Soviet ultimatum and overwhelming Soviet military strength around Berlin, the West stood firm. As time passed, Khrushchev backed off his ultimatum, and eventually withdrew it. The second Berlin crisis had passed.

Another period of improved East-West relations followed. In 1959, Khrushchev even visited the United States. However, East-West relations soon deteriorated when the U.S.S.R. shot down an American U-2 spy plane over the Soviet Union just before a U.S.-Soviet summit meeting in Paris. When U.S. President Eisenhower took responsibility for the spy flight and refused to apologize for it, Khrushchev left the summit. He refused to meet with Eisenhower again.

John Kennedy assumed the U.S. presidency in January 1961. Five months later, he met with Khrushchev in Vienna. The meeting was a disaster for the United States. Khrushchev again insisted that the West withdraw from Berlin and that the Soviet Union would sign a separate peace treaty with East Germany if need be. Once again the West stood firm, and East-West tensions escalated.

This time the crisis did not simply pass. The U.S.S.R. and East Germany had a surprise in store for the West, and for the people of Berlin. On August 13, 1961, they began to construct a wall all around West Berlin to seal it in.

There was a very pragmatic reason that the Soviets and East Germans did this. During 1961, as many as 10,000 East Germans a month defected to the West, many via Berlin. Many of the defectors, enticed by active West German efforts to recruit them, were East Germany's best and brightest people. East Germany could not survive this rate of defection for long, and the Berlin Wall — as well as increased military fortifications along the entire length of the East German-West German border — effectively plugged the gap.

Following the erection of the Berlin Wall, Berlin remained a central part of the East-West conflict. But the Berlin situation never again threatened to escalate and ignite a world war as it had in 1948, 1958, and 1961. On occasion, as in 1965, the U.S.S.R. temporarily blocked or delayed Western access to Berlin to protest Western actions.

One school of thought also argued that Khrushchev placed missiles in Cuba in 1962 to trade them for Western concessions on Berlin. There may be some legitimacy to the argument, but there is no concrete proof that this is what lay behind Khrushchev's actions in Cuba. Most analysts believe that Khrushchev attempted to deploy missiles in Cuba because the U.S.S.R. had far fewer long-range missiles than the United States, and therefore trailed in the strategic nuclear arms race.

Over time, the Berlin Wall came to symbolize the division between East and West Europe. Indeed, it became the symbol of the entire Cold War.

Coexistence and Confrontation Part II: 1962-1969

Following the Cuban Missile Crisis, neither the United States nor the Soviet Union sought confrontation. Both sides realized that the world had come to the brink of nuclear war, and neither side relished what it had glimpsed. As a result, few Cold War crises arose in Europe for much of the 1960s. Rather, both NATO and the Warsaw Pact concentrated on improving their military capabilities, with both sides hoping that those capabilities would never be used against each other.

Even so, both sides did use their military capabilities in the 1960s, the United States most obviously in Vietnam. Many European governments and peoples openly questioned the wisdom of the U.S. involvement in Vietnam, and some openly opposed it.

Even as cracks began to appear in NATO because of Vietnam, the Soviet Union undertook an action that drove NATO together again. In 1968, a new

Czechoslovakian government came to power under Alexander Dubcek. The new government vowed to turn Czechoslovakia into a multiparty state and to withdraw from the Warsaw Pact.

This was more than the U.S.S.R. could take. The Soviet Union sent its armed forces into a "fraternal socialist country" to make sure communism remained in place. Dubcek was overthrown, and the Soviet Union proclaimed the "Brezhnev Doctrine," under which the U.S.S.R. declared it had the right to intervene in communist countries to keep communism in place. Once again, a chill descended on East-West relations in Europe.

Detente in Europe: 1969-1985

The chill did not last long. President Richard Nixon took office in Washington in January 1969, pledging to move East-West relations "from an era of confrontation to an era of negotiation." Shortly thereafter, in October 1969, the Social Democratic Party won control of the German Bundestag for the first time, outpolling the long-ruling Christian Democratic Party. The Social Democrats renounced the former West German goal of unifying East and West Germany. Instead, under "Ostpolitik," they declared that West Germany now sought to work with East Germany, and would pursue a policy of reconciliation between the two.

The way was now clear to break the logjam that had deadlocked East-West relations in Europe since World War II. The first steps were taken by West Germany and the Soviet Union. In August 1970, the two states signed an agreement in which both renounced the use of force and recognized the existing borders of all states in Europe. Four months later, West Germany and Poland signed a similar treaty.

Then, in September 1972, the four countries that occupied Germany at the end of World War II — France, Great Britain, the Soviet Union, and the United States — signed a final agreement on the status of Berlin. The West conceded that West Berlin was not an actual part of West Germany, but it also received guaranteed access to the city and Soviet accession to the right to develop cultural and other ties between West Germany and West Berlin.

One final task remained. East and West Germany, in December 1972, concluded an accord that amounted to mutual recognition. Not only had the Berlin problem been solved, but so too had the German problem.

Other European problems began to be addressed in 1973. The Mutual Balanced Force Reduction (MBFR) and the Conference on Security and Cooperation in Europe (CSCE) began in 1973, and both continued into the 1980s.

MBFR was relatively straightforward, seeking to reduce the number of troops and weapons that NATO and the Warsaw Pact deployed against each other. Despite long years of negotiations, MBFR never resolved the many problems that it faced, and the military buildup in Europe continued.

CSCE was more complex. After two years of negotiations, CSCE concluded a "Final Act," signed in Helsinki in 1975 by 33 European states as well as the United States and Canada. The CSCE Final Act included three "baskets." In Basket One, all 35 states agreed to respect existing borders and not try to change them, to respect each other's sovereignty, to reject the use of force, and to settle all disputes peacefully. In Basket Two, all 35 states agreed to cooperate in economics, science and technology, and the environment. In Basket Three, all signatory states accepted a declaration of human rights that all Europeans were guaranteed. Finally, the 35 states agreed that CSCE was a continuing process, and that subsequent meetings would be held.

Since CSCE did not have any operational mechanisms, there was no way to enforce any of the Final Act's provisions or guarantees. Even so, a standard was set for governments to live up to. Indeed, many Eastern Europeans in the late 1980s attributed the changes that swept their countries then to the hope that was provided by CSCE's "Basket Three" provisions.

Between 1975 and 1985, Europe was generally outside the turbulent tides that continued to beset East-West relations. There were several exceptions to this, most notably the storm unleashed in Poland during 1980 and 1981 by the Solidarity trade union movement and the subsequent Soviet-supported Polish declaration of martial law. A storm also erupted in 1983 as NATO deployed intermediate-range nuclear forces to counter similar Soviet weapons. At the conventional military level, both NATO and the Warsaw Pact continued to improve their military forces throughout the 1970s and 1980s.

Significantly, though, none of these issues became crises that threatened general warfare. The East-West conflict and the Cold War continued, but Europe was no longer a flashpoint.

Issues for the U.S. and the World

Two of the most frequently asked questions about the Cold War are, "Who caused the Cold War?" and "Could the Cold War have been avoided?" Scholars have debated these questions for years without reaching agreement. In the SCIS Videotape "Europe After the Cold War," Background Lesson, "The Cold War in Europe," former U.S. Secretary of State Dean Rusk argues that:

1. **the Soviet Union was clearly most to blame for the Cold War.** What evidence does Mr. Rusk provide to support his position? Do you agree with his assessment? Why or why not? What evidence beyond that provided by Mr. Rusk supports your position?

2. **given Soviet policies, the Cold War was unavoidable.** What evidence does Mr. Rusk provide to support his position? Do you agree with him? Why or why not?

3. **the United States bears some of the responsibility for the onset of the Cold War**. Why does Rusk argue this? Do you agree with his position? Why or why not?

Selected Bibliography

Acheson, Dean. <u>Present at the Creation: My Years in the State Department</u> (New York: W.W. Norton, 1969).

Black, Cyril, Jonathan E. Helmreich, *et al.* <u>Rebirth: A History of Europe Since World War II</u> (Boulder, CO: Westview, 1992).

Gaddis, John Lewis. <u>The United States and the Origins of the Cold War 1941-1947</u> (New York: Columbia University Press, 1972).

Halle, Louis. <u>The Cold War as History</u> (New York: Harper & Row, 1967).

Jones, Joseph M. <u>The Fifteen Weeks</u> (New York: Viking, 1955).

Kennedy, Robert F. <u>Thirteen Days</u> (New York: W.W. Norton & Co., 1969).

Mander, John. <u>Berlin: Hostage for the West</u> (Baltimore, MD: Penguin Books, 1962).

McNamara, Robert. <u>Out of the Cold</u> (New York: Simon and Schuster, 1989).

Newhouse, John. <u>Cold Dawn: The Story of SALT</u> (Washington, DC: Pergamon-Brassey, 1989).

Rostow, W.W. <u>The Diffusion of Power: 1957-1972</u> (New York: Macmillan, 1972).

Rusk, Dean. <u>As I Saw It</u> (New York: W.W. Norton & Co., 1990).

Spanier, John. <u>American Foreign Policy Since World War II</u> (New York: Holt, Rinehart, and Winston, 1980).

Talbott, Strobe. <u>Endgame: The Inside Story of SALT II</u> (New York: Alfred A. Knopf, 1979).

Talbott, Strobe. <u>Deadly Gambits: The Reagan Administration and the Stalemate in Nuclear Arms Control</u> (New York: Vintage Books, 1985).

Yergin, Daniel. <u>Shattered Peace</u> (Boston: Houghton Mifflin, 1977).

BACKGROUND LESSON

THE COLD WAR IN EUROPE

Activity 1:

WHAT WAS THE COLD WAR?

ACTIVITY OBJECTIVE

The student will be able to distinguish among different national perspectives on the Cold War.

MATERIALS AND RESOURCES

❏ SCIS Videotape "Europe After the Cold War," Background Lesson, "The Cold War in Europe," Interview with former U.S. Secretary of State Dean Rusk

❏ Worksheet 0.1 "Cold War Questionnaire"

❏ Handout 0.1 "A Soviet Perspective on the Cold War"

❏ Handout 0.2 "A Chinese Perspective on the Cold War"

❏ Handout 0.3 "An Indian Perspective on the Cold War"

STRATEGIES

Discuss with students the idea of "perspective." Talk about how one's view may change depending on a number of factors such as age, culture, religion, political affiliation, nationality, and life experiences. Assign each student the task of asking five (or more) people the following question:

When I think of the Cold War, I think of . . .

Use Worksheet 0.1 "Cold War Questionnaire" as a means of gathering input to answer the question. In small groups, have students list key phrases used to describe the Cold War. Ask students if they can draw any generalizations from their research (e.g., effects of age, political affiliation, socioeconomic status and religion on a person's perspective). Have each group then share its key phrases and generalizations.

Remind students that they have heard several perspectives of the Cold War from people in their community. Explain that the next activity will help them to understand some perspectives of the Cold War from several different national perspectives.

Next, review the biosketch of Secretary Rusk included earlier in this educational package. Then, show the class the SCIS Videotape "Europe After the Cold War," Background Lesson, "The Cold War in Europe," Interview with former U.S. Secretary of State Dean Rusk. Discuss with students how Secretary Rusk's positions and experiences may have influenced his perspectives on the Cold War.

Select three students in the class. Give one a copy of Handout 0.1 "A Soviet Perspective on the Cold War," another a copy of Handout 0.2 "A Chinese Perspective on the Cold War," and the third a copy of Handout 0.3 "An Indian Perspective on the Cold War."

Have the students read aloud to the class the perspectives from each of these states. Discuss how the perspectives are similar or different from those of the class. Ask students how age, culture, religion, political affiliation, nationality and life experiences affect one's perspective.

Conclude the activity by having each student write an essay entitled "The Cold War: A Potpourri of Perspectives." Criteria for evaluation should be based on the student's ability to describe several different perspectives, but especially those of the United States, the former Soviet Union, China, and India.

COLD WAR QUESTIONNAIRE

1. Male _____   Female _____

2. Predominant Political Affiliation:
    Democrat _____
    Republican _____
    Other _____

3. Age: Below 15 _____   41-50 _____
         16-20 _____   51-60 _____
         21-30 _____   61-70 _____
         31-40 _____   Over 70 _____

4. Cultural Heritage: African American _____   Anglo American _____
                            Asian American _____   Hispanic American _____
                            Latino American _____   Native American _____
                            Other _____

5. Complete the following statement: "When I think of the Cold War, I think of ...

_____

_____

_____

_____

_____

_____

_____

_____

_____

_____

_____

_____

_____

_____

_____

_____

A SOVIET PERSPECTIVE ON THE COLD WAR

After World War II the principal objective of the aggressive forces in the USA was to roll back socialism and dominate the world by means of a policy of strength. Needless to say this could not fail to affect the USSR's relations with the USA. Together with other socialist countries the Soviet Union has consistently directed its efforts to erase international tension, curb the aggressors and eradicate the flashpoints of cold and hot wars . . . Another point that might be noted is that in Soviet-US relations, tension is frequently fanned by the Cold War warriors in the USA with the express purpose of preventing any normalization of possible co-operation . . .

The Soviet Union founds its policy towards the USA on the principles of peaceful coexistence, namely on principles of equality and non-interference in each other's internal affairs. However, it firmly opposes the forces of aggression and imperialism's dangerous plans.

These relations are adversely affected by US imperialism's striving to dominate the world . . . The US imperialism started an arms race and organized aggressive blocs. They began to arm the West Germans, interfere in the internal affairs of the other countries and conduct subversion against the socialist states. By their actions they launched the Cold War which they hoped would strengthen their positions and enable them to carry out their plans of aggrandizement . . . This was strikingly illus-trated by the war against the freedom-loving Vietnamese people. The atrocities per-petuated by the US military still further complicates Soviet-US relations . . .

On August 3, 1966 the Chairman of the Council of Ministers of the USSR, Alexei Kosygin . . . noted that it was the Soviet Union's unchanging stand that relations between the two countries could be improved provided the USA abided by the norms of international law and ceased its interference in the internal affairs of other coun-tries and peoples.

A Study of Soviet Foreign Policy. Progress Publishers, Moscow, 1975.

A CHINESE PERSPECTIVE
ON THE COLD WAR

The United States, the most ferocious imperialist country, has the mad strategic aim of conquering the world. It is frantically suppressing the revolutionary struggles of the oppressed peoples and nations and has openly declared its intention of bringing Eastern Europe back into its so-called world community of free nations . . . The U.S. imperialists are the wildest militarists of modern times, the wildest plotters of the new world war, and the most ferocious enemy of world peace . . .

The leaders of the CPSU (Soviet Union) are trying hard to wreck the socialist camp. They use every kind of lie and slander against the Chinese Communist Party and exert political and economic pressure on China. Hand in hand with U.S. imperialism, the Soviet Union brought pressure to bear upon revolutionary Cuba, making demands on it at the expense of its sovereignty and dignity.

The Polemic on the General Line of the International Communist Movement,
Foreign Language Press, Peking, 1968.

AN INDIAN PERSPECTIVE ON THE COLD WAR

Our country is the world's largest democracy, and it has more people than any country except China. We also have a long history and an ancient culture that goes back far longer than those of either the United States or the Soviet Union. But we are a poor country, and our armed forces could not have competed with the military of either of the superpowers.

My country won its independence from Great Britain in 1947. Almost immediately we had a civil war between Hindus and Muslims. Pakistan, which is mostly Muslim, broke away from India at the end of this war. Both because of our experience with British colonialism and the civil war, we Indians did not want to get involved in the superpower rivalry of the Cold War. We wanted to be neutral, so we helped found the Nonaligned Movement, made up of countries that wanted to stay independent from both the American bloc and the Soviet bloc.

I don't know who started the Cold War. Both sides probably did. Both sides definitely made it continue, and both sides wanted us to join their side. The Cold War was bad for the U.S. and the U.S.S.R. but it was also dangerous for the entire world. To think, two countries seriously considered that they might destroy the world because of their own disagreements. It is little wonder that many people do not like the U.S. and what was the U.S.S.R.

But as I said, India wanted to stay nonaligned. We tried, and for the most part we succeeded, although many Americans don't think so. Americans got angry with us because we wouldn't join their alliances and because we criticized them. The Soviets didn't get angry with us when we wouldn't join their alliance. They just worked with us.

I admit, we often criticized the United States, and we often disagreed with what the United States did in its foreign policy and internally. But the United States often deserved to be criticized. It is the richest country in the world, or at least it used to be. Nevertheless, it gives very little foreign aid to anyone except Egypt and Israel. It sends its military all over the world to intervene in other people's business, like Vietnam and Panama and Somalia. It sided with Pakistan during our disputes with that country. These were not and are not wise policies.

As for the Soviet Union, many of my countrymen looked at what the Soviet Union said it wanted to do — eliminate the exploitation of man by man — and liked that. But then, I am afraid, they forgot to look at what the Soviet Union really was doing. By that, I mean that as far as I am concerned, the Soviet Union was no better than the United States, and, in many ways, a lot worse. It exploited its own people, it set up its own colonial empire, it gave only limited amounts of foreign aid, and it invaded other countries too . . . not a very nice country.

Even so, India had just escaped British imperialism, was closer geographically to the Soviet Union, and had a leadership that some people say fell in love with Russia. So we probably did slant our policies toward Moscow during the Cold War a little bit. But this was understandable.

As a result, we had many Soviets who visited our country, the Kremlin gave us foreign aid, and the Soviet military sold weapons to us very inexpensively. And the Soviet Union did not demand that India join its alliance system.

The Americans would not help us at all unless we joined their treaty system. So we got aid and assistance from the Russians and got accused by the Americans of being pro-Soviet and even communist. But the Americans were wrong. We were not pro-Soviet or communist. We were just trying to do the best for our country.

All Indians are glad that the Cold War is over. It was an extremely dangerous time in the world. But the end of the Cold War did not solve our problems. We still have too many people and not enough food, not enough houses, not enough doctors. For us, the world is a lot safer with the Cold War over, but our country's situation is really not much better.

Interview of a citizen of India, conducted in Atlanta, Georgia, September 1993, by Daniel S. Papp.

LESSON 1

THE FALL OF EASTERN EUROPEAN COMMUNISM

Lesson 1 of 6 Lesson Plans for the
Southern Center for International Studies'
High School Educational Package
EUROPE AFTER THE COLD WAR

The most vivid symbol of the collapse of communism in Eastern Europe was the opening of the Berlin Wall. Here, German border guards watch demonstrators pull down one segment of the Berlin Wall.

Study Guide for

LESSON 1
of the SCIS Educational Package
EUROPE AFTER THE COLD WAR

THE FALL OF
EASTERN EUROPEAN
COMMUNISM

By the middle 1980s, communist governments had been in place in Eastern Europe for forty years. Several of the Eastern European communist governments that the U.S.S.R. installed after World War II, notably those in Hungary, Poland, and Romania, had established a certain degree of independence for themselves. The communist governments in Albania and Yugoslavia followed even more independent policies, but they were special cases since communists had risen to power there with little or no reliance on Soviet troops.

Despite Soviet willingness to tolerate a certain degree of independence in Eastern Europe, no one believed that Eastern European communist states could set completely independent courses. Soviet military actions in East Germany in 1953, in Hungary in 1956, and in Czechoslovakia in 1968 all drove home the point that there were certain undefined limits beyond which Eastern European states could not go. Soviet support for the declaration of martial law in Poland in 1981 to keep communists in place there showed the same thing.

Nevertheless, relationships between the Soviet Union and its Eastern European allies were changing. Even in the early 1980s, the Soviet Union was beginning to experience hard economic times, and a few people in the U.S.S.R. began to wonder why the Soviet Union needed so much control over Eastern Europe. This control cost the Soviet Union money, they reasoned, money that was sorely needed in the U.S.S.R. itself. Similarly, they observed, with detente proceeding nicely in Europe, the Soviet Union no longer needed Eastern Europe as a buffer zone between itself and Western Europe as it had during the Cold War.

Change was in the air. But no one expected the magnitude or rapidity of change that would sweep Eastern Europe before the end of the 1980s.

The Gorbachev Reforms

One of the people who pondered the Soviet role in Eastern Europe was Mikhail Gorbachev. Soon after he began running the Soviet Union in March 1985, he initiated a series of reforms in the U.S.S.R. that changed not only his country, but also Eastern Europe and the world.

Gorbachev's reforms began slowly. At first, he allowed the Soviet people a greater degree of freedom of expression than they ever had before. Gorbachev called this "glasnost," or "openness." Over time, he extended his domestic reforms into economics and politics as well, calling them "perestroika," or "restructuring," and "demokratizatsiya," or "democratization."

For Eastern Europe, Gorbachev's most important reforms were in foreign policy. Calling his foreign policy innovations "new thinking," Gorbachev stressed global interdependence, redefined Soviet security policy, and argued that the time had come to end military intervention outside one's own country. By 1988, Gorbachev even asserted that Eastern European countries could decide for themselves what form of government they should have.

Eastern Europeans liked what they heard, but they were skeptical. They remembered that Khrushchev had talked about "national paths toward socialism" in 1956, but when Poland and Hungary attempted to chart their own policies, they were not permitted to do so. They also remembered the invasion of Czechoslovakia in 1968. More recently, the U.S.S.R. also supported martial law in Poland in 1981.

For Eastern Europeans, then, the central question was whether Gorbachev's reforms were reality or rhetoric. The answer came in 1989.

The Revolutions of 1989

Poland and Hungary were the first Eastern European states to test the limits of Gorbachev's rhetoric. In January 1989, the Polish government and the still-illegal, non-communist trade union Solidarity began talks to end the ban on Solidarity. By March, the two agreed that open elections would be held in June. In April, the Polish government lifted the ban on Solidarity and reserved 35 percent of the seats in the lower legislative house for non-communists.

Meanwhile, in Hungary, a new constitution came into force in February 1989. It specifically rejected the "leading role" of the Communist Party. In the same month, the Hungarian government authorized the creation of a multiparty political system, the first time political parties other than the Communist Party had been allowed in Hungary in over forty years. In March, a non-communist political party, the Hungarian Democratic Forum, held a political convention.

In earlier years, these events would have led to a Soviet crackdown. But in 1989, things were different. The Soviet Union greeted these startling events with studied nonchalance. After all, Gorbachev declared, countries could determine for themselves their own governments.

The next several months brought more stunning changes. In May, Hungary, a Warsaw Pact member, began dismantling fortifications along its border with neutral, but pro-Western, Austria. It moved many of the fortifications to its border with Romania, another Warsaw Pact member, with which Hungary was embroiled in an ethnic dispute. At the same time, a reform bloc within the Hungarian Communist Party advocated that Hungary withdraw from the Warsaw Pact.

Such advocacy was one of the things that led to the Soviet invasion of Hungary in 1956, and of Czechoslovakia in 1968. This time, the Soviet Union did not respond.

In June, Poland held its elections, and Solidarity won. In August, a coalition government headed by a Solidarity Prime Minister, Tadeusz Mazowiecki, took power. Also in

August, Hungary held a free and open election that included candidates from the non-communist Democratic Forum, several of whom won.

Once again, the U.S.S.R. did nothing. Indeed, one Soviet foreign ministry spokesman even said that his country intended to replace the Brezhnev Doctrine, under which the Soviet Union claimed the right to intervene in any communist state to defend communism, with the "Sinatra Doctrine," which would allow Eastern European states to "do it (their) way." The world was amazed.

Unrest was also brewing in East Germany. In August and September, East German refugees seeking asylum crowded into West German embassies in East Berlin, Budapest, and Prague. Hungary opened its borders with Austria completely, allowing thousands of East Germans to flee there. Hundreds of thousands of East Germans took to the streets in anti-government demonstrations in East Berlin and in Leipzig.

Still, the U.S.S.R. did not intervene.

Hoping to stem popular unrest, East German leader Erich Honecker resigned in October. The new East German government opened talks with opposition leaders, but this and other concessions were not enough. In November, thousands of Berliners — East and West — simply took matters into their own hands, and marched on the Berlin Wall. Nothing was done to stop them, and the East German-West German border was opened. From this point, it was simply a matter of time before the communist East German government fell, only a month later.

Meanwhile, in late October in Czechoslovakia, police brutally broke up an anti-government demonstration in Prague. This only brought more demonstrators into the streets. After eight days of anti-government rioting in November, the communist Czechoslovakian government also bowed to the inevitable, abolishing the "leading role" of the Communist Party in government, and initiating wide-ranging reforms, including the acceptance of non-communist participation in government. By December, the Czechoslovakian communist government was a thing of the past.

So too were communist governments in Bulgaria and Romania. In Bulgaria, long-time leader Todor Zhivkov resigned in November. The following month, the Bulgarian Communist Party renounced its right to rule. In Romania, after troops and police fired on demonstrators, the Romanian people rose up against their communist government and killed or arrested its leaders.

With the Romanian revolution, every Soviet-installed communist government in Eastern Europe was gone. Communism lingered on in Albania until 1990 and in parts of Yugoslavia into 1993 as that unfortunate country fragmented and then collapsed into a deadly civil war.

By the end of 1989, then, Eastern Europeans had their answer. Gorbachev's reforms were real, not just rhetoric.

Eastern Europe After Communism

The euphoria that swept Eastern Europe in late 1989 and early 1990 was short-lived. Very quickly, the peoples of Eastern Europe realized that they had an immense challenge ahead of them. The task of constructing new societies would not be easy. One of the most difficult tasks resulted from the fact that no country had ever tried to do what the Eastern European states were about to try: dismantle centralized communist economic, political, and social institutions, and create free market economic systems, democratic political systems, and open social systems.

The challenge was made even more difficult by the fact that in many countries, the elimination of communism was less than complete. In some states, despite the fall of communist governments, individuals who wanted to continue to do things the old ways remained very influential. Often, they sought to retain as much of the old system as possible. The emergence of right wing fascist and neo-Nazi groups in Eastern Europe also complicated the task of creating free market economic systems, democratic political systems, and open social systems.

In addition, the Soviet Union still had troops in Czechoslovakia, East Germany, Hungary, and Poland. All these countries wanted the U.S.S.R. to withdraw its troops. Negotiations between Moscow and the new Eastern European governments began soon after the new governments assumed power, and in all cases, the U.S.S.R. agreed to withdraw its forces. The East German case was particularly interesting since West Germany agreed to build troop barracks for the U.S.S.R. in the Soviet Union so that Soviet troops would have a place to live when they were withdrawn from East Germany.

Despite the successful negotiations on the withdrawal of Soviet troops, immense problems lay ahead for every Eastern European state. How much would it cost to convert to capitalism and to rebuild industries that had been neglected for years? Where would the money come from to do this? After over forty years of communism, could Eastern Europeans still operate successfully in a capitalist society? If not, could they learn, and how long would it take? Could the needed political, economic, and social institutions so requisite to the functioning of a democratic society and a free market economy be grafted successfully onto the remnants of communism? What social, ethnic, and other problems that had been dormant under the harshness of communist rule would bubble to the surface? How much human suffering would take place as the transition from communism and autocracy to capitalism and democracy was made?

Some countries fared better than others. East Germany was perhaps the most fortunate. It had long been the dream of many Germans, perhaps most Germans, to unite into a single country. In fact, the objective of unification of Germany was included in the West German constitution. Now, they had their chance. On October 3, 1990, the two parts of Germany again became one country. With West Germany's extensive wealth, East German economic reconstruction could also move forward relatively quickly, at least in comparison to other former communist Eastern European states. Even so, immense problems remained in the former East Germany.

In Poland, the post-communist political scene saw Lech Walesa, the leader of the Solidarity labor movement that had become a political party, come to power. However, Solidarity was not the only political party in the country. Communists remained influential, and far-right politicians gained in influence as well. By 1993, democracy was the political order of the day in Poland, but the situation remained unstable.

Despite the unstable political scene in Warsaw, Walesa's government moved ahead quickly with free market economic reforms termed "shock therapy." In its basic conception, shock therapy included removing subsidies, eliminating price controls, devaluing Polish currency, and introducing a balanced government budget. At first, the Polish standard of living, already low, dropped precipitously. By 1993, however, Poland's economic free-fall appeared to have stopped. Some observers even detected an upturn.

Hungary's political scene was even more divided than Poland's, with over 60 parties taking part in the 1990 elections. However, only 7 received enough votes to obtain seats in the new Hungarian Parliament, and Hungary made the transition to a Western-style democracy in good order.

Hungary also faced sizeable economic problems. However, unlike Poland, the Hungarian government did not opt for shock therapy. It pursued a moderate course of reform, maintaining some government subsidies and keeping some price controls. Nevertheless, the Hungarian government's objective was to institute a free market economy in the near future.

The transition to a democratic government went smoothly in Czechoslovakia, where noted dissident writer Vaclav Havel was elected president. Czechoslovakia faced economic problems, but it became apparent that the country's greatest challenge was to remain a single country. Despite Havel's efforts to maintain unity, Czechoslovakia, in 1993, peacefully split into two, the Czech Republic and Slovakia. Albania, Bulgaria, and Romania all faced similar political, economic, and social problems.

By 1993, it remained unclear in much of Eastern Europe what the final results of the revolutions of 1989 would be. But it was clear that the task of reconstructing Eastern Europe — now known in many circles as "Central Europe" — would be long and arduous. The task of building new societies would not be easy.

Issues for the U.S. and the World

The countries of Eastern Europe have changed significantly since the end of World War II, going from countries dominated by the Soviet Union to independent states. The transition has been from communism toward capitalism, and from autocracy toward democracy. These transitions have not been easy, nor are they complete. In the SCIS Videotape "Europe After the Cold War," Lesson 1, "The Fall of Eastern European Communism," the former Secretaries of Defense raise several issues regarding these transitions. The issues the former Secretaries raise include:

1. **the reasons for increasing tension in Eastern Europe despite the end of the Cold War**. Why does former Secretary Schlesinger claim that tensions are rising in Eastern Europe? What could be done to counter rising tensions?

2. **U.S. aid to Eastern Europe.** Do the Secretaries believe that the U.S. should send aid to Eastern European states? Why or why not? What are some of the arguments that could be used against the Secretaries' positions?

3. **the need to build an infrastructure in Eastern Europe.** The former Secretaries observed that one reason that the Marshall Plan was successful was because an infrastructure was already in place in Western Europe. In

contrast, Eastern European states do not have such infrastructures. According to the Secretaries, what kind of assistance would be helpful to these countries? What role should other countries play in helping Eastern European states?

4. **methods through which transitions from communism and autocracy to capitalism and democracy can best be accomplished**. Different Eastern European states have tried different approaches to make the transition from communist and autocratic societies to capitalist and democratic ones. What is meant by "shock therapy" reforms tried in Poland? What approach did Hungary try? How successful were these and other Eastern European reforms?

Selected Bibliography

Gorbachev, Mikhail. <u>Perestroika: New Thinking for Our Country and the World</u> (New York: Harper and Row, 1987).

Mason, David S. <u>Revolution in East-Central Europe: The Rise and Fall of Communism and the Cold War</u> (Boulder, CO: Westview, 1992).

Patterson, Perry L. (Editor), <u>Capitalist Goals, Socialist Past: The Rise of the Private Sector in Command Economies</u> (Boulder, CO: Westview, 1993).

Schopflin, George. <u>Politics in Eastern Europe 1945-1992</u> (Cambridge, MA: Blackwell, 1993).

Serafin, Joan. (Editor), <u>East-Central Europe in the 1990s</u> (Boulder, CO: Westview, 1993).

Simons, Thomas W. <u>Eastern Europe in the Postwar World</u> (New York: St. Martins, 1991).

Staar, Richard F. (Editor), <u>East-Central Europe and the USSR</u> (New York: St. Martins, 1991).

Stokes, Gale. <u>The Walls Came Tumbling Down: The Collapse of Communism in Eastern Europe</u> (New York: Oxford University Press, 1993).

Szakolczai, Arpad, and Agnes Horvath. <u>The Dissolution of Communist Power: The Case of Hungary</u> (New York: Routledge, 1992).

Wandycz, Piotr S. <u>The Price of Freedom: A History of East-Central Europe from the Middle Ages to the Present</u> (New York: Routledge, 1992).

LESSON 1

THE FALL OF EASTERN EUROPEAN COMMUNISM

Activity 1:

EASTERN EUROPE IN THE EARLY 1990S

ACTIVITY OBJECTIVE

The student will be able to describe the sequence of events that led to the current situation in Eastern Europe.

MATERIALS AND RESOURCES

❑ Worksheet 1.1 "Research Query Sheet"

❑ Handout 1.1 "Timeline of Recent Events in Eastern Europe"

❑ Current news sources, almanacs, political and geographic handbooks

STRATEGIES

Since the 1989 revolutions ousted Eastern European communist governments from power, many new governments in the region have been moving toward free market economies and democratic political systems. Unfortunately, most are experiencing severe social, political, and economic problems.

In order to determine the current status of these states, divide the class into six groups. Assign each group one of the following countries: Hungary, Poland, Czechoslovakia (which peacefully split into Slovakia and the Czech Republic in 1993), East Germany (which became part of Germany in 1990), Bulgaria, Romania or Yugoslavia (which split into several countries in 1992 and has since been torn by warfare).

Distribute Worksheet 1.1, "Research Query Sheet," to each group. Provide students with time in the media center or provide current almanacs, atlases, political and geographic handbooks, computer data bases, and other reference materials in the classroom. Allow time for each group to gather the background information on their assigned country. Make sure that each group member has a completed Research Query Sheet for his/her country.

Distribute Handout 1.1, "Timeline of Recent Events in Eastern Europe." Explain to students that they should examine the timeline and identify all of the entries that pertain to the country that they are researching. Encourage them to examine all of the entries and list any items that affect their country. For instance, after the division of Yugoslavia, students will need to look for Slovenia, Croatia, Bosnia and Macedonia. Students will also need to watch for other entries about Russia, the European Community, etc. Then each group should create a timeline of events for their assigned country. If possible, have the students put the timelines on long strips of paper, such as newsprint or bulletin board paper. Encourage students to use the same increments of time so that the timelines can be placed on a wall or bulletin board for comparison. Allow time for each group to share the timeline and explain what has happened in the country in recent years. Discuss with students similarities and differences between states. Students may also want to periodically update the timeline from current news sources.

After students have become "experts" on their particular country, have them write a political platform for a new political party forming in the Eastern European country that they studied. Criteria for evaluation should include:

- knowledge of background information, including geographic, economic, social, political and historical content.
- appreciation of the cultural heritage of the country.
- knowledge of the chronology of events since 1989.
- knowledge of the current political challenges facing the country.

RESEARCH QUERY SHEET

The Fall of Eastern European Communism

Use a variety of sources from the media center to locate the following information on your country.

I. Background
> Official name of country
> Capital of country
> Area in square miles/kilometers
> Type of government
> Chief Executive (name and title)
> Brief biography of chief executive
> List and briefly describe other key leaders since 1988.

II. Geography
> List countries and bodies of water that border your country.
> List and describe major physical or geographic features that affect the country.

III. Economics
> List major crops, natural resources, and industries.
> List Monetary Unit and current rate of exchange.
> List Gross National Product, Per Capita GNP, Exports and Imports.

IV. Social
> Describe the major ethnic groups, religions, languages, life expectancy and literacy rate.

V. Political
> Identify the major political parties and their goals.
> Describe the legislative, executive and judicial branches.

VI. History
> Give a BRIEF history of the country, including specific factors that are affecting the current situation.

VI. Challenges
> List and briefly describe five key problems and challenges currently facing this state.

TIMELINE OF RECENT EVENTS
IN EASTERN EUROPE

1989

January 11	Yugoslavia: The government and party leadership resign after mass demonstrations led by the Serbian leader Slobodan Milosevic.
February 6	Poland: Government and Solidarity begin official talks.
February 11	Hungary: Government creates a multiparty political system (first in 40 years).
March 13	Romania: Reports published that six retired officials had written a letter of protest to Ceausescu.
March 26	USSR: Partially free elections bring many dissidents into the new Parliament.
April 7	Poland: Agreement to lift ban on Solidarity and the government reserves 35 percent of the seats in the lower legislative house for non-communists.
May 2	Hungary: Begins dismantling fortifications along the borders with Romania.
May 8	Hungary: Janos Kadar forced to retire as party president.
May 17	Czechoslovakia: Havel released from jail after being arrested in January for commemorating Jan Palach's suicide in 1969.
June 4	China: Deng Xiao-ping sends tanks into Beijing's Tiananmen Square to break up demonstrations.
	Poland: Holds elections and Solidarity wins.
July 6	France: In a speech to the Council of Europe Gorbachev says, "Any interference in domestic affairs and any attempt to restrict the sovereignty of states . . . is inadmissible."
August 21	Czechoslovakia: Small demonstration on the anniversary of the 1968 invasion is broken up by police.
August 24	Poland: Solidarity leader Tadeusz Mazowiecki is elected as the first non-communist prime minister in Eastern Europe.
September 10	Hungary: Border with Austria is opened to any East Germans who wish to leave. Thousands leave during a four-day period.
October 7	East Germany: Celebration of East Germany's 40th anniversary. Anti-communist demonstrations in the streets are broken up by police. Demonstrations continue.
October 9	East Germany: Police are ordered to disperse a demonstration of 70,000 in the streets of Leipzig. The order is canceled at the last minute.
October 18	East Germany: Longtime Communist President Erich Honecker resigns. The new East German government opens talks with opposition leaders.
October 25	Finland: Gorbachev announces that the Brezhnev Doctrine is dead. He affirms that the USSR has no right to interfere in the affairs of its neighbors.

November 3	Bulgaria: Police break up demonstration during an international environmental conference.
November 7	East Germany: The existing government resigns.
November 9	East Germany: East German government announces that the borders between East and West Germany are open. The Berlin Wall is opened for transit between East and West Berlin.
November 10	Bulgaria: Communist Party leader Todor Zhivkov is replaced by reform communist leader Petar Mladenov.
November 17	Czechoslovakia: In Prague an anti-government demonstration is broken up by police.
November 18	Bulgaria: Mass demonstration demanding free elections.
November 20	Czechoslovakia: Extremely large demonstrations continue in Prague.
November 24	Czechoslovakia: Alexander Dubcek returns from exile and enters Prague as a hero. Milos Jakes and the rest of the communist Politburo resign.
November 26	Hungary: People reject the government's proposal for a presidential election.
November 27	Romania: Ceausescu is reelected to a five-year term as the Communist Party leader.
November 27	Czechoslovakia: Two-hour general strike is staged to show support for democracy.
November 28	Czechoslovakia: Communist Party promises free elections.
December 3	East Germany: Central Committee and Politburo resign.
December 7	Czechoslovakia: Communist government resigns.
December 10	Czechoslovakia: President Gustav Husak resigns and a new non-communist majority government is formed.
December 14	Romania: Demonstrations begin against Ceausescu.
December 17	Romania: Many people killed in Timisoara by police acting on Ceausescu's orders to stop all demonstrations.
December 19	Croatia, Yugoslavia: Free elections are slated for 1990.
December 21	Romania: Ceausescu is shouted down at a pro-government rally.
December 22	Romania: Revolution breaks out. Demonstrators seize the government buildings and Ceausescu tries to escape, but is later caught. Chaos continues.
December 24	Slovenia, Yugoslavia: Free elections approved for 1990.
December 25	Romania: National Salvation Council orders Ceausescu tried and shot.
December 28	Czechoslovakia: Dubcek elected as Chairman of National Assembly.
December 29	Czechoslovakia: Vaclav Havel elected President of Czechoslovakia.

1990

January 1	Poland: Introduction of economic reforms including end of price controls and subsidies.
	Yugoslavia: Currency becomes tied to the German deutschmark.
January 15	Bulgaria: Free elections promised for June 1990.
January 22	Yugoslavia: Yugoslav Communist Party splits.
January 28	Poland: Polish Communist Party dissolves.
January 29	East Germany: Erich Honecker is arrested.
January 30	USSR: Gorbachev concedes to German unification.
February 1	Bulgaria: Government resigns. Alexander Lilov becomes party leader.
February 3	Romania: A coalition takes over after the government resigns.
March 15	East Germany: Christian Democrats win 48% of the vote in the first free elections since 1932.
March 25	Hungary: Non-communist government selected in elections.
April 3	Bulgaria: Bulgarian Communist Party changes its name to Socialist Party.
April 8	Slovenia, Yugoslavia: Non-communist government wins 80% in election.
April 12	East Germany: New coalition government takes control.
April 22	Croatia, Yugoslavia: Communists defeated in elections.
May 18	East Germany: Treaty signed with West Germany merges their currencies under the West German mark, effective July 1. A market economy will be established in East Germany in July.
May 20	Romania: Ion Iliescu and the National Salvation Council win presidential and parliamentary elections.
May 27	Poland: Local elections cast out communists throughout the country.
June 8	Czechoslovakia: Civic Forum wins parliamentary elections.
June 10	Bulgaria: Non-communist party (Socialist) wins elections.
July 1	East and West Germany: Monetary union is achieved, using the West German mark.
July-August	Romania: Led by students, Romanians continue to protest against Iliescu's National Salvation Front, and against high prices and food shortages.
July 6	Bulgaria: Mladenov resigns.
July 13	Albania: 4,000 Albanians arrive in Italy seeking political asylum.
July 20	Czechoslovakia: Government ends subsidies on most foods.
September 12	Germany: In the Two-Plus-Four Treaty with East and West Germany, the Four Powers promise full sovereignty to the unified Germany on October 3.
October 1-2	Yugoslavia: Nationalist tensions escalate across Yugoslavia after Croatia declares itself autonomous and Serbia annexes Kosovo.
October 3	Germany: East and West Germany are unified.
December 2	Germany: Voters throughout Germany elect Helmut Kohl (CDU: conservative) as the first Chancellor of united Germany.
December 9	Poland: Walesa beats Polish-Canadian businessman Tyminski in runoff elections.

December 18	Albania: After widespread unrest, opposition forms a new political party.
December 21,23	Yugoslavia: Slovenia and Croatia vote for independence and demand a confederation within Yugoslavia.

1991

January 7	Czechoslovakia: Government receives a $1.8 billion loan from the IMF.
February	Croatia: Continues to take steps toward independence from the federal Yugoslav government.
February 20	Slovenia: Parliament amends its constitution, invalidating federal Yugoslav laws in Slovenia.
February 25	Eastern Europe: Agreement is reached to formally abolish the Warsaw Pact in July.
April 1	Romania: Government ends food subsidies. Prices double.
April 6	East Germany: First day of open travel between Poland and East Germany is marred by neo-Nazi demonstrations; two Poles are injured.
April 15	The European Bank for Reconstruction and Development (EBRD) is created to provide support as Eastern and Central European countries move toward market economies. The European Community pledges $23 billion in aid.
May 22	Poland: Solidarity demands an end to wage restraints and removal of all communists from government.
May 30	Croatia, Yugoslavia: Parliament authorizes secession from Yugoslavia if an agreement cannot be worked out.
June 19	USSR: Last Soviet troops pull out of Hungary and Czechoslovakia.
June 23	Yugoslavia: US Secretary of State favors preserving the country of Yugoslavia.
June 25	Yugoslavia: Croatia and Slovenia declare independence from Yugoslavia. Europeans are split over whether or not to recognize the new nations.
June 26	Croatia: Fighting breaks out between Croats and ethnic Serbs.
June 28	USSR: COMECON, the Soviet trade alliance of communist states, is abolished.
July 1	Eastern Europe: The Warsaw Pact is formally abolished at a summit in Prague.
July 2	Croatia: Fighting continues.
July 14	Bulgaria: A new constitution is put into effect by the communist-led government guarantees both human and property rights. Opposition groups protest.
August 7	Yugoslavia: A cease-fire ends as ethnic Serbs shell a village in Croatia.
August 19	USSR: Opposition leaders to the reforms in the USSR attempt a coup d'etat and hold President Gorbachev under house arrest.

August 22   USSR: Attempted coup fails; Yeltsin emerges as a hero.

August 25   Yugoslavia: Serbian forces attack Croatia.

September 6 EC: The European Community announces a plan to encourage free access for goods from Hungary, Czechoslovakia and Poland; plan is blocked by France.

September 18 Yugoslavia: Macedonian Parliament votes to seek independence from Yugoslavia.

September 26 Romania: Premier Petre Roman and his cabinet resign because of rioting of coal miners protesting economic reforms.

October 13   Bulgaria: The Socialists (formerly the Communists) lose power to the right-of-center Union of Democratic Forces.

October 17   Western Europe: NATO announces cut of 80% in its nuclear arsenal.

Yugoslavia: Yugoslav army starts offensive in several parts of Croatia.

October 22   Czechoslovakia: President Havel signs political and trade agreements with U.S.; Czechoslovakia appeals for U.S. investment.

October 27   Poland: Holds first fully democratic election; 42.5% of the population votes.

October 29   Poland: President Lech Walesa offers to serve as own Prime Minister.

November 4   Bulgaria: Filip Dimitrov of the Union of Democratic Forces becomes Prime Minister.

November 8   Yugoslavia: EC and U.S. place economic sanctions on Yugoslavia.

November 17 Croatia: After enduring a three-month siege from Serbian forces, the Croatian town of Vukovar falls.

December 3   Yugoslavia: EC restores trade to the former Yugoslav republics of Croatia, Slovenia, Macedonia, and Bosnia-Herzegovina, but continues sanctions against Serbia and Montenegro.

December 5   Poland: President Lech Walesa nominates defense lawyer Jan Olszewski as Prime Minister. Poland and the USSR sign a friendship agreement the next day.

December 6   Yugoslavia: Another Yugoslav/Croatian cease-fire collapses.

December 8   USSR: Leaders of Russia, Ukraine, and Belarus meet in Minsk, proclaim the death of the USSR, and propose a "Commonwealth of Independent States" instead.

December 10 Romania: Country approves a new Constitution with a multiparty presidential republic.

December 11 Czechoslovakia: Parliament passes a law providing prison terms for anyone convicted of promoting communism or fascism.

December 11 EC: Leaders agree on a treaty creating central bank and single currency by 1999, establishment of common foreign and defense policies. This is the Maastricht Treaty.

Bulgaria: Parliament approves law confiscating Communist Party property.

December 16 EC: Poland, Czechoslovakia, and Hungary sign a ten-year agreement with the EC, granting them trade and economic assistance.

December 17 EC: Will recognize Croatia and Slovenia on Jan. 15; Germany to recognize on Dec. 25.

December 25   USSR: Mikhail Gorbachev announces his resignation as
                         Soviet President.
December 26   USSR: The Soviet parliament formally votes itself out of existence.

1992

January 2   Germany: Former East German secret police files opened.
January 3   Yugoslavia: A UN-mediated cease-fire is agreed upon by Serbia
                         and Croatia.
January 9   Yugoslavia: Serbs in Bosnia and Herzegovina proclaim autonomy.
January 15   Yugoslavia: Slovenia and Croatia recognized as independent states
                         by EC.
January 19   Bulgaria: Zhelyu Zhelev of the Union of Democratic Forces is elected
                         President. Blaga Demitrova becomes the first woman Vice President
                         in post-communist Eastern Europe.
February 14   Macedonia: Over 200,000 Greeks demonstrate against possible EC
                         recognition of Macedonian independence from Yugoslavia.
February 21   Croatia: The UN agrees to send peacekeeping forces to Croatia.
February 27   Czechoslovakia: Germany and Czechoslovakia sign treaty giving
                         German support to Czechoslovakia's entry to EC.
March 1   Yugoslavia: Bosnia-Herzegovina votes to seek independence from
                         Yugoslavia. Some native Serbs in Bosnia initiate violence.
March 5   Poland: Parliament rejects government plan to slow move toward
                         free market.
March 18   Poland: Government completes austerity budget.
April 5   Germany: Far right parties score big gains in local German elections.
April 6   Bosnia: EC recognizes independence of Bosnia-Herzegovina;
                         Serbs continue to bomb Bosnia.
                     Germany: German political leaders vow to solve immigration
                         problem by creating an immigration policy.
April 7   Poland: Rumors focus on possible coup by the military; some ascribe
                         undemocratic intentions to President Lech Walesa.
April 25   Germany: 2.5 million public service workers go on strike for
                         higher wages.
May 2   Bosnia: Serbian attack on Sarajevo escalates into an all-out war.
May 8   Poland: Lech Walesa asks for stronger executive powers; says
                         instability scares off foreign investment.
May 18   Czechoslovakia: Government begins selling off state-owned
                         companies to citizens.
May 30   Yugoslavia: UN Security Council votes 13 to 0 for economic sanctions
                         on Yugoslav government.
June 4   Yugoslavia: Elections result in a victory for Milosevic.
June 5   Poland: Parliament votes to dismiss PM Jan Olszewski; elects
                         Waldemer Pawlek as the 4th PM in less than three years.
June 20   Czechoslovakia: Czechs and Slovaks agree to split Czechoslovakia
                         into two separate countries.

June 23   Bosnia: Croatian troops attack Serb-controlled territory in Yugoslavia.

July 2   Yugoslavia: Milan Panic leaves the U.S. to become the PM of Yugoslavia.

July 3   Czechoslovakia: Parliament rejects reelection of President Vaclav Havel.

July 5   Bosnia: Croatian nationalists declare own independent state in Bosnia-Herzegovina.

July 8   Poland: Lech Walesa nominates Hanna Suchocka as Poland's new PM.

July 20   Germany: Eases immigration policy toward Bosnians.

July 29   Germany: Former East German leader Erich Honecker is flown to Germany from Russia to face corruption and manslaughter charges.

August 7   Bosnia: Serbian forces continue to shell Sarajevo.

August 21   Bosnia: Serbian leaders pledge to close prison camps; mortar shells continue to pound Sarajevo.

August 29   Germany: Thousands of Germans demonstrate against the racial violence that has been taking place.

August 30   Poland: Government dismisses striking employees of state-run enterprises.

September 4   Bulgaria: Former communist leader Zhirkov convicted of embezzlement, sentenced to prison.

September 5   Germany: Right wing militants attack refugee shelters.

September 22   Yugoslavia: The UN expels Yugoslavia.

September 25   Bosnia: Envoys report a new wave of "ethnic cleansing."

September 27   Romania: Parliamentary and presidential elections held; runoff expected.

September 30   Romania: Election Bureau declares 15% of ballots illegal.

October 12   Romania: President Ion Iliescu wins Romanian elections with over 60% of the vote.

October 24   Bosnia: Serbs and Croats step up attacks on the Muslims in Bosnia.

October 28   Poland: Last Russian troops leave Poland.
   Bulgaria: Government resigns after losing vote of confidence.

November 4   Romania: President Iliescu names Nicoleau Vacaroiu PM.

November 23   Germany: German right wingers firebomb house, killing 3 Turks.

November 25   Czechoslovakia: Parliament ratifies division of country at the end of 1992.

December 2   Germany: Government bans songs of several neo-Nazi rock groups.

December 13   Bosnia: Another Bosnian cease-fire signed.

December 17   Poland: Coal miners go on strike to protest government plan to cut 180,000 mining jobs.

December 20   Yugoslavia: Slobodan Milosevic wins Serbian election; Milan Panic claims widespread voting fraud.

December 29   Yugoslavia: Communists and Nationalists combine in Yugoslav Parliament for no-confidence vote against PM Milan Panic.

December 30:   Bulgaria: Parliament names Lyuben Berov PM.

1993

January 1	Czechoslovakia: Peacefully separates into Czech Republic and Slovakia.
January 2	Bosnia: Leaders of five Bosnian factions begin talks in Geneva on partitioning Bosnia.
January 8	Hungary: State radio and television leaders resign, saying they can no longer protect industry from growing government influence.
January 23	Yugoslavia: Five months after Serbia agrees to shut down detention camps, US intelligence says 135 still open.
January 25	Slovenia: New coalition government elected with ex-communists retaining most posts.
January 26	Czechoslovakia: Vaclav Havel elected to five-year term as president of Czech Republic.
January 27	Slovakia: Lawmakers fail to elect a president.
February 2	Bosnia: UN mediators Cyrus Vance and Lord Owen complain that U.S. reluctance to back their peace plan severely hinders ending war in Bosnia.
February 6	Bosnia: Serbs accelerate "ethnic cleansing" in eastern Bosnia.
February 10	U.S. government gives support to the Vance-Owen Bosnian peace plan.
February 15	Slovakia: Parliament elects Michal Kovac first President.
March 3	Bosnia: UN High Commission for Refugees says Serb forces are carrying out a massacre of Muslims in eastern Bosnia.
March 18	Poland: Parliament defeats a bill to privatize 600 state companies.
March 29	Croatia: Government resigns because of economic problems.
March 31	Bosnia: UN Security Council authorizes NATO forces to shoot down planes violating "no-fly zone" over Bosnia.
April 14	Hungary: Government bans use of all Nazi and Communist symbols.
April 17	Russia: Government tells U.S. it will not support tighter sanctions on Serbia.
May 6	Bosnia: UN Security Council votes to establish Sarajevo, Tuzla, Iva, Gorazde, Bihac, and Srebrenica as "safe zones" free from attack.
May 23	Bosnia: Bosnian President Alija Izetbegovic declares new Western plan for "safe zones" totally unacceptable; urges people to fight on.
May 28	Poland: Government of Hanna Suchocka collapses after losing no-confidence vote.
May 28	Germany: Five members of a Turkish family are burned to death in a blaze set by neo-Nazis.
June 16	Germany: Chancellor Helmut Kohl announces a plan to ease restrictions on German citizenship.
July 1	Bosnia: UN officials say they have strong evidence of close cooperation between the Serb and Croat forces against the Bosnian Muslims.

July 9	Bosnia: The Bosnian government rejects a plan to divide the country into three ethnic states.
July 22	Bosnia: Serb forces shell Sarajevo so heavily that the Bosnian government delays a new round of peace talks in Geneva.
July 28	Bosnia: The U.S. says it will help bomb Serb positions around Sarajevo as soon as the UN requests such action.
August 2	Bosnia: Bosnian President Alija Izetbegovic breaks off peace talks because of Serbian attacks near Sarajevo.
August 28	Bosnia: Bosnia's parliament rejects U.N. peace proposal to divide Bosnia into three parts.
September 8	Bosnia: In meetings in Washington, U.S. rejects Bosnian President Alija Izetbegovic's plea for assistance.
September 16	Germany: Three former East German leaders convicted in Berlin of inciting border guards to kill citizens fleeing to West.
September 20	Poland: Results from Poland's parliamentary elections indicate former communists will lead left wing coalition in next government, with 173 of 460 total seats.
September 20	Bosnia: Meeting to sign latest Bosnian peace accord cancelled after negotiations deadlock.
September 29	Bosnia: Bosnian parliament votes to accept partition plan but only if territories seized by Serbs and Croats are returned.
October 20	Albania: Albania becomes first former Eastern European communist state to sign military aid agreement with U.S.
December 12	Hungary: Prime Minister Jozef Antall dies, leaving Hungarian political leadership unclear.
December 20	Serbia: Socialist Party claims victory in parliamentary elections.
December 29	Bulgaria, Romania, and Germany: Bulgaria expels Russian right wing leader Vladimir Zhirinovsky; Romania and Germany deny him entry.

LESSON 1

THE FALL OF EASTERN EUROPEAN COMMUNISM

Activity 2:

WHAT PROBLEMS DOES EASTERN EUROPE CURRENTLY FACE?

ACTIVITY OBJECTIVE

The student will be able to identify significant problems that exist in Eastern Europe today.

MATERIALS AND RESOURCES

❑ SCIS Videotape "Europe After the Cold War," Lesson 1, "The Fall of Eastern European Communism"

❑ Current news sources, <u>National Geographic</u> magazines, almanacs

❑ Worksheet 1.2 "Problem Solving Format"

STRATEGIES

Copy and distribute the biographies of the former Secretaries of Defense, found at the front of "Europe After the Cold War." Have students read the biographies. Discuss the events that took place in Eastern Europe when each Secretary was in office. Have the students discuss how these events may have influenced each Secretary's view of Eastern Europe.

Have students watch the SCIS Videotape "Europe After the Cold War," Lesson 1, "The Fall of Eastern European Communism." As they watch the videotape, have them list all of the problems that the former communist Eastern European states currently face. Discuss some of the problems and possible solutions voiced by the former Secretaries of Defense.

Divide the class into small groups. Have each group conduct research to determine other problems faced by Eastern Europe today (or refer to the Research Query Sheet, Worksheet 1.1). Students will need to be guided to include problems such as environmental issues, property ownership, infrastructure, currency, investment, unemployment, elections, etc.

After students have listed the problems, have them prioritize the list and choose one problem for further research. Provide a variety of sources to enable students to gather data on the problem. Students may want to contact new immigrants from the region or experts in the community, if available. After students have thoroughly researched one of the problems, distribute Worksheet 1.2, "Problem Solving Format." Have each group complete the format. Encourage them to consider a variety of alternatives and to brainstorm solutions as mentioned by the secretaries. Allow students time to share their solutions with the class.

Criteria for evaluation should include:

- Working cooperatively and productively within a group
- Statement and explanation of a relevant problem.
- Explanation of possible solutions that are reasonable and show in-depth thought and research
- Description of the consequences of the possible solutions
- Determination of a plausible solution(s) based on the consequences listed on the chart.

PROBLEM SOLVING FORMAT

STATEMENT AND EXPLANATION OF THE PROBLEM

POSSIBLE SOLUTIONS

A	B	C	D

CONSEQUENCES

A1	B1	C1	D1

A2	B2	C2	D2

A3	B3	C3	D3

RECOMMENDED SOLUTION(S) AND EXPLANATION

LESSON 2

THE EUROPEAN UNION

Lesson 2 of 6 Lesson Plans for the
Southern Center for International Studies'
High School Educational Package
EUROPE AFTER THE COLD WAR

AP Wide World Photo, Inc.

Can Europe ever become unified? The European leaders who concluded the Maastricht Treaty in December 1991 think so. They included, from the left of the front row: Premier Silva, Portugal; President Mitterand, France; Queen Beatrix, Netherlands (whose country hosted the meeting, but who did not herself participate in the negotiations); Premier Major, Britain; Premier Schluter, Denmark. Second row, from the left: Premier Mitsotakis, Greece; Chancellor Kohl, Germany; European Community President Delors; and Premier Gonzalez, Spain.

Study Guide for

LESSON 2
of the SCIS Educational Package
EUROPE AFTER THE COLD WAR

THE EUROPEAN UNION

Even as Eastern European peoples were trying to remake their societies, twelve Western European countries were attempting to integrate and unify their political, economic, social, and foreign and defense policies to form the equivalent of a "United States of Europe." This Western European experiment, called the European Community (EC), was in many respects as difficult a challenge as the one that Eastern Europe was undertaking.

Until recently, the EC was an entity that concentrated primarily on reducing barriers to trade and other forms of interchange between its twelve member states. But in 1991, leaders of the European Community concluded an agreement, the Maastricht Treaty, that made economic and political unity the EC's ultimate objective.

By late 1993, all of the EC member states had ratified the Maastricht Treaty, and on November 1, 1993, the EC formally became the European Union (EU). Like the EC before it, the major parts of the EU are the European Economic Community (EEC); the European Coal and Steel Community (ECSC); and the European Atomic Energy Commission (EURATOM).

Here, it may be useful to differentiate between "integration" and "unity" as they applied to the EC, and now to the EU. "Integration" was the process of reducing barriers to trade and other forms of interchange between the EC's twelve members, and of creating EC-wide political and economic institutions that could aid in this process. When the EC evolved into the EU in 1993, this process of integration had proceeded a long way.

"Unity," by comparison, was and is the objective of having all EC/EU states have common political, economic, social, foreign and security policies, that is, of creating a true "United States of Europe." Despite the change in name from the EC to the EU, and despite the considerable progress that has been made on European integration, neither the EC nor the EU achieved unity.

Indeed, many people in Western Europe and elsewhere argue that the divisions that remain between and among the twelve EU states are so great, so sharp, and so deeply imbedded that unity will not be achieved. Others assert that even if greater European integration proves possible, unity is not desirable. Nevertheless, the EC has become the EU, and efforts to increase European integration so that unity can be achieved continue.

The Beginning of European Integration

Western Europe has come a long way on the road toward greater cooperation between and among the twelve EU states. The road toward greater cooperation between the twelve has often been difficult and complex.

For centuries, the different ethnic and nationality groups of Europe had fought each other over different political, economic, social, ethnic, religious, cultural, and territorial disputes. On occasion, as during World Wars I and II, European disagreements had embroiled the entire world. It was understandable that after World War II, many Europeans believed that a way had to be found to prevent future wars in Europe.

At the same time, the damage that World War II caused in Europe had destroyed the economy of most European countries. Economic production was virtually nonexistent in much of Europe, and human suffering was immense. Europe's economic destruction was so complete that a way had to be found to "jump start" the economy of an entire continent, not just a country or two.

The need to jump start Europe's economy was paralleled by the U.S. and Western European fear that in the absence of European economic improvement, the Soviet Union and communism would find fertile ground for expansion into Western Europe. From the U.S. and Western European perspectives, this had to be prevented.

With these political, economic, human, and strategic objectives in mind, European and U.S. leaders began to cast about for a policy idea that would address all these concerns. One idea that appeared to have merit was creating an integrated and more unified Europe.

As early as September 1946, British Prime Minister Winston Churchill urged that French-German reconciliation be undertaken within the framework of "a kind of United States of Europe." To Churchill, this would integrate the German and French economies so that future warfare between the two would be unlikely, accelerate economic growth in the two war-ravaged countries, and create a political-economic counterbalance to the Soviet Union.

At first, nothing was done about Churchill's suggestion. However, the entire European economy continued to languish. Indeed, in February 1947, Great Britain informed the U.S. that its economic situation was so serious that it could no longer provide aid to either Greece or Turkey.

The U.S. acted, and in four short months between March and June 1947 proposed both the Truman Doctrine and the Marshall Plan. Under the Truman Doctrine, U.S. President Harry Truman promised that the U.S. would provide assistance to "free people" struggling against internal enemies or externally sponsored subversion. Under the Marshall Plan, U.S. Secretary of State George Marshall offered U.S. economic assistance to Europe for a collective European Recovery Plan.

After Marshall's offer, events proceeded slowly but relentlessly. After several meetings, one of which included the Soviet Union before it walked out, European states requested aid from the U.S. The U.S. Congress at first did not act, but following the February 1948 communist coup in Czechoslovakia, it agreed to fund part of the European request. In April 1948, Western European states signed a treaty creating the Organization for European Economic Cooperation to administer Marshall Plan aid, which began to flow later in 1948. The U.S. eventually provided over $15 billion in economic aid to Western Europe under the Marshall Plan.

Three points must immediately be made. First, the Marshall Plan was widely regarded, with good reason, as an extremely generous and humanitarian U.S. action. British Prime Minister Winston Churchill once called it the most generous act in human history.

Second, the U.S. provided Marshall Plan aid not only for humanitarian reasons, but also because it was in U.S. economic and security interests to do so. Marshall Plan aid helped restore Europe as a trading partner, and helped combat communist influence in Western Europe.

Third, the Marshall Plan was undertaken on the basis of European governments jointly studying their problems and their needs, jointly developing a program to address those problems and needs, jointly requesting funds from the United States to undertake their program, and jointly administering and implementing the program. In effect, the Marshall Plan was the first step down the road toward European integration.

The next major step toward European integration was the European Coal and Steel Community, proposed by French Foreign Minister Robert Schuman in May 1950. Under the ECSC, all Western European coal and steel production would be placed under one administering authority. In 1951, Western European states concluded such a treaty.

Further steps toward European economic integration took place in June 1955 when West Germany, France, Italy, the Netherlands, Belgium, and Luxembourg decided to cooperate even more fully on economic issues. Then, in March 1957, representatives from the same countries signed the Treaties of Rome, which created the European Economic Community (EEC) and EURATOM. In 1962, economic cooperation was extended to agriculture, and Greece associated itself with the growing European organization. Two years later, Turkey received associated status. By 1968, all industrial tariffs between EEC members were eliminated. The EEC also removed limitations on movement of workers among member countries, and established a common external tariff. Europe had moved a long way down the road toward economic integration since 1945.

Since 1968, the European Community (EC) has expanded to twelve members with the addition of Denmark, Great Britain, Greece, Ireland, Portugal, and Spain. Equally important, in 1979, EC member states held the first direct election for the 410-member European Parliament. In addition, during the 1980s, all 12 of the EC's members agreed to accept the decisions of the EC's governing body, the European Council, on certain issues even if they as states disagreed with them. This in effect transferred limited sovereignty from the 12 EC member states to the EC. The states even agreed to allow the EC to determine what each owed the EC, in effect giving the EC limited taxation powers. Clearly, European integration was proceeding apace.

European Economic Integration:
The Single European Act

More impressive steps on the path toward Western European integration were still to come. Fearing that the EC was lagging behind the United States and Japan economically, European leaders in 1985 passed the Single European Act. This act set the end of 1992 as the time when all barriers within the EC on the movement of goods, capital, and people between countries would be eliminated. About 300 different regulations were eliminated.

Implementation of the Single European Act at the end of 1992 made Western Europe the single largest trading market in the world, surpassing even the United States.

The advantages that the Act offered Europe can best be illustrated by a single example. In 1988, truck drivers in Western Europe needed as many as 27 separate documents to go from one country to another. In 1993, all they needed was their driver's license.

This is not to say that the Single European Act did not have problems. One of the major issues was whether the EC should be "deepened" or "broadened" first. Advocates of deepening asserted that before more states were brought into the EC, thereby broadening it, the EC should be more fully integrated, that is, the parameters of cooperation among present members should be deepened. Conversely, advocates of broadening asserted that if the EC were truly to become a European Community, then more European states, including the newly non-communist states of Eastern Europe, should be welcomed into the organization.

Other concerns addressed what the Single European Act would do to EC members. Many states feared — and fear — that inexpensive labor in Greece, Portugal, and Spain will attract capital there and lead to unemployment elsewhere. They were — and are — also fearful that immigrants from Eastern Europe, North Africa, or elsewhere may move to Western Europe and take many jobs at lower wages than Western Europeans are willing to work for.

In addition, some states were concerned — and remain concerned — that Germany's economic strength might give it too much clout within the EC. They fear that German products and German capital may crowd their own national products and capital out of their own countries, thereby making the EC simply a way for Germany to become more powerful and influential.

And many other people in every EC country saw — and see — a danger that European Community bureaucrats will make decisions and impose standards from their headquarters in Brussels that will eliminate local decision-making and national culture throughout Europe.

Outside Europe, some countries also expressed concern about the impact that European economic integration might have on them. For example, despite being a longtime supporter of European integration, the United States feared that once the EC eliminated all internal barriers to trade, the EC might impose high external tariffs to keep non-European products outside the EC. This would reduce U.S. exports to Europe, thereby hurting the U.S. economy. The U.S. also feared that EC governments would subsidize production of certain goods within their own countries, thereby artificially reducing the cost to consumers. This too would hurt U.S. exports to

Europe, and to other parts of the world.

By 1993, the U.S. concern about high European tariffs had substantially disappeared. The EC assured the U.S. that it had no intention of raising tariff barriers, and for the most part, it had not. But the U.S. concern about European subsidies had become a major issue, especially in agriculture and aircraft. In both areas, the U.S. claimed that European governments were providing large subsidies to producers, thereby undercutting U.S. prices, reducing what U.S. producers could sell, and hurting the U.S. economy. The two sides negotiated, and by 1994 resolved several of their differences. Nevertheless, disagreements remained.

European Political and Economic Unity: The Maastricht Treaty

Despite these internal European and external U.S. concerns about the future of European integration, European leaders met in Maastricht, the Netherlands, in December 1991 and forged an agreement that went far beyond the Single European Act. The agreement, called the Maastricht Treaty, envisioned the EC moving beyond integration and on to political and economic union, creating a virtual "United States of Europe."

The Maastricht Treaty was ambitious. It proposed that the twelve EC members would: 1.) join together in a political and economic union; 2.) adopt a single common currency; 3.) share the same set of policies on social and domestic issues; and 4.) have a common foreign and defense policy. In short, the Maastricht Treaty sought to create a true United States of Europe.

But Europe's leaders had moved too far too quickly. Gradually, opposition to the Maastricht Treaty built. Before the treaty could become operational, each EC country had to approve it according to its own laws. Soon it became apparent that despite the support of European leaders, rank-and-file Europeans were less willing to move quickly toward European unity.

In June, 1992, Danish voters defeated the Maastricht Treaty. In September, French voters approved it by one percent. In November, after a bitter fight, the British Parliament approved a procedural matter on the Treaty by a narrow margin. The Maastricht Treaty was in trouble.

The difficulties that the Maastricht Treaty encountered increased debate in Europe about the future of the European Community and the wisdom of unity. Before the Maastricht Treaty, most discussions about the EC centered on economic issues and the economic advantages — and dangers — that the EC might bring about. After Maastricht, many discussions also explored a more fundamental question, namely, "Should the EC lead to European unity, and what exactly does European unity imply for the sovereignty of my country and the future of Europe?"

Much of the opposition to the Maastricht Treaty resulted from the same issues that caused concern about the Single European Act — capital flight to countries where labor was inexpensive, immigrants willing to work for low wages, German economic domination, EC bureaucratization, and the imposition of too many European-wide standards. However, two other issues also played a major role in building opposition to the Maastricht Treaty: a single currency and nationalism.

The currency issue centered on the Maastricht Treaty's intention to create a single European-wide currency. Many Europeans simply did not want to give up their traditional currency — the pound, the frank, the mark, and so on. They saw the intention to create an EC monetary unit as an assault on their own nationality, and as increasing the possibility that their own national economies would be dominated by the country with the strongest economy, Germany.

Thus, the currency issue was closely connected with the second issue, nationalism. Many Europeans had developed a "European consciousness," that is, a sense that they were part of a greater Europe. However, many others had not. To them, European unity meant that their country would lose its own separate national identity, its sovereignty, and its sense of nationhood. To many people, this simply was not acceptable.

But others concluded that separate national identities could be protected within a united EC. Thus, when, in 1993, Danes were given a second chance to vote on the Maastricht Treaty, one of the major issues was whether Denmark could remain Danish within a united EC. When votes were counted, Denmark had approved the treaty. Later in the year, Great Britain approved the treaty, with the significant caveat that it would not abide by EU decisions in social policy.

In November 1993, then, with all of its members having approved the Maastricht Treaty, the EC evolved into the EU. Many questions remained about the future of the EU, including the question of whether or not there would be a single European currency and whether or not common social, foreign, and defense policies could be created. Nevertheless, even if true unity had not yet been achieved, European integration had proceeded a long way since the Marshall Plan.

Issues for the U.S. and the World

In the SCIS Videotape "Europe After the Cold War," Lesson 2, "The European Union," the former Secretaries of Defense and State address the questions of an integrated and unified Europe, and what the concepts mean for U.S. policy. Also, the Secretaries point out that from the U.S. perspective, NATO is especially important since, from its creation, it has been the basis for strong formal ties between the United States and Western European states. In their discussions, the former Secretaries raise questions and explore issues related to:

1. **the future of European integration.** Despite the plans set forth in the Single European Act, European integration has not yet been achieved. In the videotape, Donald Rumsfeld and George Shultz offer their ideas as to why integration has been so difficult to achieve. What reasons do they put forward? What are the differences between European integration and European unity?

2. **European integration and economic realities**. One purpose of European integration was to enhance economic conditions in all EC states. However, some states may benefit more than others as economic integration proceeds, and some even believe that economic integration may harm their economies. Secretaries Muskie and Haig identify some of the economic costs that further integration may incur. What are they? Are there any other costs that may be incurred? How can these potential costs be weighed and balanced against the potential benefits?

51

3. **European integration and the transitions in Eastern Europe.** As initially envisioned, European integration was to apply only to Western Europe. However, with the transitions taking place in Eastern Europe, several Eastern European states have expressed interest in becoming members of the European Community. What are the pros and cons of this, from both the Western European and the Eastern European perspectives?

4. **U.S. interests regarding an integrated Europe.** Secretary Weinberger addresses the U.S. position regarding an integrated Europe, and what this might mean for the relationship between the United States and its European allies. Why does he believe that it is important for the United States to remain linked to Europe?

Selected Bibliography

Cafruny, Alan W., and Glenda G. Rosenthal. The State of the European Community, Volume 2: The Maastricht Debates and Beyond (Boulder, CO: Lynne Rienner Publishers, 1993).

Delors, Jacques. Our Europe: The Community and National Development (New York: Routledge, 1992).

Dinan, Desmond. Ever Closer Union? An Introduction to the European Community (Boulder, CO: Lynne Rienner, Publishers, 1994).

George, Stephan. Politics and Policy in the European Community (New York: Oxford University Press, 1991).

Goodman, S.F. The European Community (New York: St. Martins, 1990).

Hurwitz, Leon, and Christian Lequesne. (Editors), The State of the European Community: Policies, Institutions, and Debates in the Transition Years (Boulder, CO: Lynne Rienner Publishers, 1991).

Keohane, Robert O., and Stanley Hoffman. (Editors), The New European Community: Decisionmaking and Institutional Change (Boulder, CO: Westview, 1991).

Laffan, Brigid. Integration and Co-operation in Europe (New York: Routledge, 1992).

Milward, Alan S. The European Rescue of the Nation-State (Berkeley, CA: University of California Press, 1993).

Smith, Dale L., and James Lee Ray. (Editors), The 1992 Project and the Future of Integration in Europe (New York: M.E. Sharpe, 1992).

Story, Jonathon. The New Europe: Politics, Government, and Economy Since 1945 (Cambridge, MA: Blackwell, 1993).

LESSON 2

THE EUROPEAN UNION

Activity 1:

WHAT ARE THE PROS AND CONS OF EUROPEAN INTEGRATION AND UNITY?

ACTIVITY OBJECTIVE

The student will be able to understand and analyze issues related to European integration and unity.

MATERIALS AND RESOURCES

❑ Worksheet 2.1 "Perspectives on European Integration and Unity"

❑ SCIS Videotape "Europe After the Cold War," Lesson 2, "The European Union"

❑ Europe 2000: The Road to European Union, The Foreign Office of the Federal Republic of Germany, Public Relations Department, 5300 Bonn (if available).

❑ Europe, Our Future: The Institutions of the European Community, 2100 M Street, NW, Suite 707, Washington, DC 20037, (202) 862-9500 (if available).

STRATEGIES

Assign students to groups of four and provide one copy of Worksheet 2.1 "Perspectives on European Integration and Unity" per group. Explain to students the difference between "European integration" and "European unity." Ask members in each group to number off from 1 to 4, and be responsible for one of the following assignments:

> 1= U.S. perspective supporting European integration and unity
> 2= U.S. perspective opposing European integration and unity
> 3= European perspective supporting European integration and unity
> 4= European perspective opposing European integration and unity

Show students the SCIS Videotape "Europe After the Cold War", Lesson 2, "The European Union," which includes a discussion by the former U.S. Secretaries of Defense and Secretaries of State on the topic of European integration and unity. As students watch the tape, they should summarize the points which support or oppose the process of integration and the process of unity from their assigned perspective.

The videotape addresses at least five different issues that can be mentioned prior to starting the tape:

1. Defense of Europe and promotion of world peace
2. "Fortress Europe" versus balance of trade among world trading blocs
3. Immigration and the question of regional inclusion/exclusion in the EC
4. Sovereignty and the question of national identity
5. Disparity between the "have" and "have not" European nations

When students finish watching the tape, each group should discuss the above issues and complete Worksheet 2.1 with a summary of various positions based on individual assignments. In the case of the "European perspective" students should try to construct the relative positions based on inferences from the former Secretaries. Each group member is responsible for learning the pros and cons of both perspectives during the process.

Randomly call on members of different groups to write one pro and/or con rationale on the chalkboard (flip chart or overhead transparency may be preferable) until all rationales are included. Then, as a class, discuss Robert McNamara's initial point that "the structure of Europe and the relationship among the European nations is for the Europeans to decide." Should the U.S. have any say in this matter, and if so, what should the U.S. position be?

In summary, have all students write a one-page paper explaining what the U.S. position should be regarding European integration and unity.

PERSPECTIVES ON EUROPEAN INTEGRATION AND UNITY

In four-person groups number off from 1 to 4. As each group watches the videotape, the 1's will write down all the statements that seem to support integration and unity from a U.S. perspective, the 2's will summarize those points that oppose integration and unity from a U.S. perspective, and the 3's and 4's will do the same thing from a European perspective.

PERSPECTIVES	PRO	CON
UNITED STATES		
EUROPE		

ISSUES

The following issues are discussed in the context of remarks made by former Secretaries of Defense or Secretaries of State. Summarize how each relates to European integration and unity.

1. Defense of Europe and promotion of world peace

2. "Fortress Europe" versus balance of trade among world trading blocks

3. Immigration and question of regional exclusion/inclusion in EC

4. Sovereignty and the question of national identity

5. Disparity between the "have" and "have not" European nations

LESSON 2

THE EUROPEAN UNION

Activity 2:

WHAT IS THE EUROPEAN COMMUNITY?

ACTIVITY OBJECTIVE

The student will understand the history of the development of the European Community.

MATERIALS AND RESOURCES

❑ Handout 2.1 "The Major Treaties"

   Part 1: "The Schuman Plan"

   Part 2: "The Treaty of Rome"

   Part 3: "The Single European Act of 1985"

❑ U.S. History textbooks

STRATEGIES

Before its November 1993 transition into the European Union, the European Community was an institution that sought to enhance the political and economic integration of Europe. In many ways, it succeeded.

Explain to students that what was the European Community (EC), and what is now the European Union (EU), is composed of several institutions: the European Economic Community (EEC), the European Coal and Steel Community (ECSC), and the European Atomic Energy Commission (EURATOM). In contrast to other similar organizations, (e.g., the United Nations), the EC in some areas has received the power from its member states to exercise authority over policy issues, just like a national government. These powers, however, are not universal, but rather are restricted to specific fields defined in the treaties.

The idea of European integration has been around a long time, but the actual process began shortly after World War II. With regard to the changing face of the EC and EU, "integration" should be viewed as a process that brings the states of Europe closer together, while "unification" should be viewed as the objective that the EU is seeking. Nevertheless, this does not mean under "unification," individual states will necessarily dissolve and become part of a larger European entity.

To trace the history of this process, students will analyze three major treaties leading up to the Maastricht Treaty of 1991, which will be covered in Activity 3. Place students into groups of three and assign each member one of the following excerpts to read and to teach to the other members of the group: "The Schuman Plan," Handout 2.1, Part 1; "The Treaties of Rome," Handout 2.1, Part 2; and "The Single European Act of 1985," Handout 2.1, Part 3. Have students read the specified selection and then answer the Who? What? When? and Why? questions about their treaty. If necessary, pair up members from different groups having the same excerpt to compare notes and prepare visuals to assist in their presentations.

Part 3 contains excerpts from the Single European Act. Have students assigned to this handout discuss why this document was such an important treaty in moving toward European integration.

Group members should choose the two or three most salient points about their treaties to share with their other two members. Allow 3-5 minutes per treaty in each group. Then randomly call on students to describe important points about each of the treaties leading up to Maastricht.

Compare the Luxembourg Declaration, discussed under the Treaties of Rome, with the U.S. Constitutional Convention of 1787. Ask the following question to focus on the common problem of both bodies:

> **How did each political body address the issue of representation of the larger states relative to the smaller states?**

If students are not familiar with the "Great Compromise" made at the Constitutional Convention of 1787, provide U.S. history textbooks for them to access such information.

THREE MAJOR TREATIES

Part 1 – The Schuman Plan

After World War II Winston Churchill called for the creation of a European political union, in essence a "United States of Europe." However, governments that were recovering from the economic ravages of war were not prepared to grant other states co-determination in important national policy decisions. Beginning in 1948, economic cooperation among European states began to grow through the administration of Marshall Plan economic aid from the United States. Yet, it was not until 1950 that Europe took its own fledgling steps toward economic integration. Surprisingly, it would start with the cooperation of two archenemies, France and Germany. The proposal was known as the Schuman Plan.

French Foreign Minister Robert Schuman announced that the French Government was prepared to form a common policy with the German Government in the coal and steel sector. What made this gesture so sensational was that it had been only five years since these two countries had been at war with one another, and now they were pursuing a joint venture in an area which had served as the foundation for the armaments industry. The plan culminated in 1951 with the establishment of the European Coal and Steel Community (ECSC), which was soon joined by four other countries (i.e., Italy and the three Benelux countries of Belgium, the Netherlands and Luxembourg).

The immediate economic goal of the EC was to create a competitive market without national tariffs or quotas, but the long-range political goal was to bind the states so closely together economically that war among them would become unthinkable and impossible. This strategy did much to reduce old rivalries, particularly that between France and Germany.

THREE MAJOR TREATIES

Part 2 – Treaties of Rome

In 1957 the six European Coal and Steel Community (ECSC) countries met in Rome to create the other two communities associated with European economic integration: the European Economic Community (EEC), sometimes referred to as the Common Market, and the European Atomic Energy Commission (EURATOM). While EURATOM enabled greater cooperation and harmony in the field of atomic energy, the EEC aimed at the elimination of all internal tariff barriers, the development of a common tariff system with respect to the outside world, and the free movement of labor and capital among member states. Like the ECSC, the EEC (or Common Market) became a rapid success in Europe.

By 1965 the major bodies performing the tasks of the three Economic Communities included the **European Council** (of Heads of State and Government), the **Council of Ministers**, **the European Commission, the European Parliament,** and **the Court of Justice.** The Council of Ministers served as the executive branch of the EC. In the beginning (through the end of 1965) almost all the Council decisions were to be unanimous. All member states were to stand unanimously behind each and every resolution passed. Unanimity protected the smaller states from resolutions that might be imposed upon them by larger states, but at the same time, it gave small European countries the ability to prevent or delay decisions or compromises regarding integration. So, beginning in 1966, majority rule decisions were to replace unanimity in many areas.

It was anticipated that smaller states would suffer being overruled in such controversial areas as agricultural subsidies and tariffs. The **Luxembourg Declaration** of 1966 was an attempt to deal with this impasse. The member states agreed on an alternative that if a pending majority decision were to be completely unacceptable to one country, then the decision would not be made until a solution were sought to which all countries could then agree. The result was that many times votes would not be taken by the Council even though decisions could have been pushed through with majority votes. Though the Luxembourg Declaration never acquired the legal status of other EC treaties, it continued to be respected by the Council for many years. This also slowed down European integration considerably because experimental programs were never tried due to lack of consensus.

THREE MAJOR TREATIES

Part 3 – The Single European Act of 1985

Signed in 1986, this treaty increased the powers of the European Parliament and set the stage for the EC's 1992 Program – an ambitious plan designed to eliminate all remaining barriers to the completion of a unified market by the end of 1992. The Single European Act designated the creation of a "European Union" as the culmination of this unification process. While not the same as "The United States of Europe" envisioned by Winston Churchill, the European Community moved into the 1990s with a plan for economic, political and social integration. What follows are some excerpts from this treaty:

> Moved by the will to continue the work undertaken on the basis of the Treaties establishing the European Communities and to transform relations as a whole among their States into a European Union, in accordance with the Solemn Declaration of Stuttgart of 19 June 1983 . . .

> Determined to improve the economic and social situation by extending common policies and pursuing new objectives, and to ensure a smoother functioning of the Communities by enabling the institutions to exercise their powers under conditions most in keeping with Community interests . . .

> Have decided to adopt this Act . . .

> #### Article 1

> The European Communities and European Political Cooperation shall have as their objective to contribute together to making concrete progress towards European unity.

> #### Article 2

> The European Council shall bring together the Heads of State or of Government of the Member States and the President of the Commission of the European Communities. They shall be assisted by the Minister for Foreign Affairs and by a Member of the Commission.

> In order to promote its overall harmonious development, the Community shall develop and pursue its actions leading to the strengthening of its economic and social cohesion.

> In particular the Community shall aim at reducing disparities between the various regions and the backwardness of the least-favored regions.

LESSON 2

THE EUROPEAN UNION

Activity 3:

WHAT EFFECT HAS THE MAASTRICHT TREATY HAD ON EUROPE?

ACTIVITY OBJECTIVE

The student will develop an understanding of the issues of European unification that the Maastricht Treaty raises.

MATERIALS AND RESOURCES

❑ Handout 2.2 "Selected Text from the Maastricht Treaty"

❑ Worksheet 2.2 "The Maastricht Treaty"

❑ Handout 2.3 "Maastricht Treaty Key"

❑ Worksheet 2.3 "Case Studies on the Maastricht Treaty"

> "French Wine Producer (page 1)"
> "British Clothier (page 2)"
> "Turkish Immigrant to Germany (page 3)"
> "Mercedes Benz Auto Mechanic (page 4)"
> "Hotel Manager in Italy (page 5)"

STRATEGIES

After the passage of the Single European Act, the next step for the EC was the Maastricht Treaty, which among other things seeks to create a common European currency, a European Central Bank, a common foreign and defense policy, political unity, social equality, and labor relations. (See Handouts 2.2 and 2.3 for an explanation of these topics.) After the Maastricht Treaty was approved by all twelve EC states, the EC renamed itself the European Union (EU), even though difficulties remained in attaining many of these objectives.

Divide the class into five groups and distribute to each group one copy of Handout 2.2 "Selected Text from the Maastricht Treaty" and Worksheet 2.2 "The Maastricht Treaty." Have students read the excerpts, discuss the major points, and fill in the worksheet boxes what the treaty says under each listed topic. Discuss with the class what information they put in the boxes as well as how this treaty differs from previous ones. Then distribute the key (Handout 2.3) and discuss any differences or confusing terms mentioned by each group. Distribute to each group one of the case studies from Worksheet 2.3 "Case Studies on Maastricht." Announce that the groups must answer the questions at the bottom of the case studies and be prepared to discuss their positions with the rest of the class. Advise students that they will need to apply the information from Handouts 2.2 and 2.3 in order to answer the questions.

Allow each group 5 minutes to present the Case Study to the class and to explain its position on Maastricht ratification. Assessment should be based on group cooperation and shared presentation, validity of answers relative to the points in the Maastricht Treaty, and the clarity of the oral presentation.

SELECTED TEXT FROM THE MAASTRICHT TREATY

(signed in Maastricht, February 7, 1992)

Article A

By this Treaty, the High Contracting Parties establish among themselves a European Union, hereinafter called 'the Union.'

Article B

The Union shall set itself the following objectives:

–   to promote economic and social progress which is balanced and sustainable, in particular through the creation of an area without internal frontiers, through the strengthening of economic and social cohesion and through the establishment of economic and monetary union, ultimately including a single currency in accordance with the provisions of this Treaty;

–   to assert its identity on the international scene, in particular through the implementation of a common foreign policy, which might in time lead to a common defense;

–   to strengthen the protection of the rights and interests of the nationals of its Member States through the introduction of a citizenship of the Union;

–   to develop close cooperation on justice and home affairs;

Article G

The Treaty establishing the European Economic Community shall be amended in accordance with the provisions of this Article, in order to establish a European Community.

A –   Throughout the Treaty:

(1)   The term 'European Economic Community' shall be replaced by the term 'European Community.'

B. –   In Part One 'Principles':

(2)   Article 2 shall be replaced by the following:

Article 2

The Community shall have as its task, by establishing a common market and an economic and monetary union and by implementing the common policies or activities referred to in Articles 3 and 3a, to promote throughout the Community a harmonious and balanced development of economic activities, sustainable and non-inflationary growth respecting the environment, a high degree of convergence of economic performance, a high level of employment and of social protection, the raising of the standard of living and quality of life, and economic and social cohesion and solidarity among Member States.

Article 3a

1. For the purposes set out in Article 2, the activities of the Member States and the Community shall include, as provided in this Treaty and in accordance with the timetable set out therein, the adoption of an economic policy which is based on the close coordination of Member States' economic policies, on the internal market and on the definition of common objectives, and conducted in accordance with the principle of an open market economy with free competition.

2. Concurrently with the foregoing, and as provided in this Treaty and in accordance with the timetable and the procedures set out therein, these activities shall include the irrevocable fixing of exchange rates leading to the introduction of a single currency, the ecu, and the definition and conduct of a single monetary policy and exchange-rate policy, the primary objective of both of which shall be to maintain price stability and, without prejudice to this objective, to support the general economic policies in the Community, in accordance with the principle of an open market economy with free competition.

3. These activities of the Member States and the Community shall entail compliance with the following guiding principles: stable prices, sound public finances and monetary conditions, and a sustainable balance of payments.

Article 3b

The Community shall act within the limits of the powers conferred upon it by this Treaty and of the objectives assigned to it therein.

In areas which do not fall within its exclusive competence, the Community shall take action, in accordance with the principle of subsidiarity, only if and in so far as the objectives of the proposed action cannot be sufficiently achieved by the Member States and can therefore, by reason of the scale or effects of the proposed action, be better achieved by the Community.

THE MAASTRICHT TREATY

General Provisions – EC

Economic/Monetary Union

Maastricht
Treaty

Political Unity –

Labor Relations –

Social Equality –

MAASTRICHT TREATY KEY

General Provisions – EC

acquires authority to act over a broad range of topics ranging from foreign affairs, environment, health and tourism. To avoid charges of undue internal interference, the EC adopts the idea of "subsidiarity" in which it may act only where objectives cannot be better achieved by individual states.

Economic/Monetary Union

Commits EC to create a central bank and single currency by 1/1/97 if a majority of members have achieved "convergence" measured in terms of inflation, interest rates, budget deficit and currency stability. Otherwise, it will be created automatically on 1/1/99 by those meeting requirements.

Maastricht Treaty

Approved in December, 1991 to go into effect January, 1993 but has suffered setbacks on ratification due to nationalistic concerns. Directives or laws require unanimous approval of member states; but treaty defines numerous areas where decisions will be made through majority vote. In these cases, voting powers are weighted to favor the more populous nations.

Political Unity

Creates the status of European "citizen." As such, community nationals can live and work anywhere in Europe as well as vote and run for election in local or European Parliament elections. It aims to give EC a voice in foreign affairs and common defense.

Labor Relations

Members signed agreement (not UK) to promote and standardize working conditions, supporting workers' health and safety; gender equality in pay scales and job opportunities, social security, unemployment, & labor-management relations.

Social Equality

A separate protocol annexed to the treaty commits the EC to bridge the gap in living standards between the richer and poorer members by channeling extra resources to those countries with a GNP less than 90 percent of the community average.

CASE STUDIES ON THE MAASTRICHT TREATY

French Wine Producer

You are Claude Jonpier, owner of a small vineyard and wine exporting business. Your family has made wine for generations and is fiercely proud of its traditional quality and independence. Your father was killed during the Nazi occupation while fighting for the resistance. For this reason you have always harbored a mistrust of the Germans. You are very concerned about the acid rain which has reduced the productivity of the vineyards in recent years. Your wine has generally sold well throughout Europe even though it has to compete with domestic varieties. You would like to increase exports to include the large U.S. market but have met with political resistance in the form of tariffs.

1. Which parts of the Maastricht Treaty would most likely work to your benefit? Why?

2. With which sections of the treaty would you have serious concerns? Why?

3. How do you feel that your country should have voted in regard to the Maastricht Treaty? Explain your answer.

CASE STUDIES ON THE MAASTRICHT TREATY

British Clothier

You are Rachel Belchamp, who immigrated to the British Isles from Jamaica in the late 1970s. At age 50 you now manage a respectable clothing store in London which has survived foreign imports based on tariffs and a good understanding of British consumer tastes. You miss former Prime Minister Margaret Thatcher, who you felt represented your interests and politics the best. You are concerned about immigrants coming in to sell cheap clothing that does not measure up to British standards. Since your whole life savings are tied up with the store, you are concerned about inflation and currency depreciation. The less tax on your goods and business, the better.

1.   Which parts of the Maastricht Treaty would most likely work to your benefit? Why?

2.   With which sections of the treaty would you have serious concerns? Why?

3.   How do you feel that your country should have voted in regard to the Maastricht Treaty? Explain your answer.

CASE STUDIES ON THE MAASTRICHT TREATY

Turkish Immigrant to Germany

You are Ahmed Muhammed, 17 years old and unemployed. You have lived in Munich, Germany all of your life and speak fluent German and Turkish. Your parents moved to Germany from Turkey just before you were born. They still live and work in Germany, but they do not wish to lose their national, ethnic, and religious ties to Turkey. You would like to use some of your technical training in the construction business if you had the chance to work. You have heard of persecution by "Skinheads," but have not seen it yourself. Germany is your home. However, you would be willing to move anywhere in Europe that provided a job and security. You also like the German health care system, especially since you are planning to have a family someday.

1.   Which parts of the Maastricht Treaty would most likely work to your benefit? Why?

2.   With which sections of the treaty would you have serious concerns? Why?

3.   How do you feel that Germany should have voted in regard to the Maastricht Treaty? Explain your answer.

CASE STUDIES ON THE MAASTRICHT TREATY

Mercedes Benz Auto Mechanic

You are Christopher Schultz, a 27-year-old auto mechanic in the Mercedes plant in Stuttgart, Germany. You are concerned that Mercedes auto production is down due to the recession after unification. Although you recognize that German auto workers are the highest paid in the world, life for your wife and children is harder now that you are facing higher taxes to reconstruct the former East German economy. Because you have only been employed two years, you have little seniority if there are cutbacks at the plant. You feel somewhat betrayed by Chancellor Helmut Kohl, who promised that unification could be achieved with no additional tax burden on the West. Now, there is talk about diverting resources to other poorer members of the EC. You know that you and other German workers have the best government- and industry-provided social support programs in the world, but you would like more done for the German workers.

1.   Which parts of the Maastricht Treaty would most likely work to your benefit? Why?

2.   With which sections of the treaty would you have serious concerns? Why?

3.   How do you feel that your country should have voted in regard to the Maastricht Treaty? Explain your answer.

CASE STUDIES ON THE MAASTRICHT TREATY

Hotel Manager in Italy

You are Maria Bertolini. You and your husband Luigi together manage a small hotel on the coast just outside the city. Most of your business is made from German and French tourists in the summer. You would like to expand, but it is just too expensive right now. It is difficult to cater to some of your customers because there is not the selection of fresh produce and meats available at affordable prices. You recently put in a satellite dish, but not all the rooms have been wired yet. Skilled technicians are not easily found in this community. At age 42 with two grown children, it is time to plan for retirement, but there is no money. You are concerned about what European unification will do to your business.

1. Which parts of the Maastricht Treaty would most likely work to your benefit? Why?

2. With which sections of the treaty would you have serious concerns? Why?

3. How do you feel that your country should have voted in regard to the Maastricht Treaty? Explain your answer.

LESSON 3

NATIONALISM
IN EUROPE

Lesson 3 of 6 Lesson Plans for the
Southern Center for International Studies'
High School Educational Package
EUROPE AFTER THE COLD WAR

In 1989, demonstrators in Prague, Czechoslovakia, used nationalism to overthrow the communist government and expel Soviet influence. Two years later, Czech and Slovak nationalism led to the peaceful separation of Czechoslovakia into the Czech Republic and Slovakia, two independent states.

Study Guide for

LESSON 3
of the SCIS Educational Package
EUROPE AFTER THE COLD WAR

NATIONALISM
IN EUROPE

Despite movement toward greater integration and even unity in Western Europe, nationalism remains an important force in European affairs. It is what binds the French together as France, the Germans together as Germany, and the Danes together as Denmark. It is what makes each nationality proud of its own national heritage and its own country.

Unfortunately, nationalism is also the force that in many respects led to World Wars I and II. It is the same force that has led to the brutal war in the former Yugoslavia among Croats, Serbs, and Muslim Slavs.

Given the continuing importance of nationalism in Europe — and the world — today, and given the range of what nationalism can do and is doing in Europe and beyond, it is vitally important that we understand what nationalism is, where it came from, and where it may be going.

State, Nation, Nation-State, and Nationalism

Until recently, the term "nation" was used almost interchangeably with "state" and "nation-state." It was never correct to do this, but nevertheless, it was widely done.

This is changing. The breakup of Czechoslovakia, the Soviet Union, and Yugoslavia, and the nationality difficulties that Belgium, Canada, Great Britain, India, Russia, and other states throughout the world are having make it extremely important that the differences between these terms are understood.

A state is an area of the earth's surface that has human-created boundaries. A state is governed by a central authority that makes laws, rules and decisions that it enforces within those boundaries. A state makes its own policies, and the government of a state recognizes no earthly authority higher than itself within its own boundaries.

A nation need not necessarily control an area of the earth's surface, nor need it necessarily have a government or make policy. A nation is simply a group of people who see themselves linked to one another in some manner. Groups of people who consider themselves to be ethnically, culturally, or linguistically related may thus be considered a nation. In essence, a nation is a psychological fixation as much as anything else.

A nation-state is a state whose inhabitants consider themselves to be a nation. It is an area of the earth's surface with human-created boundaries under a single government, the population of which considers itself to be in some way, shape, or form, related.

Nationalism is closely related to the concepts of nation and nation-state. In simplest terms, nationalism is the psychological force that binds together people who identify with each other. Nationalism refers to the feelings of attachment that members of a nation have to one another and to their nation-state.

Nationalism has both positive and negative dimensions. As a positive force, nationalism leads people to have a sense of pride about themselves, their nation, and their nation-state, if they have one. As a negative force, nationalism may lead members of one nation to slaughter members of another.

When is a state a nation-state? Sometimes that is an easy question to answer. For centuries, Denmark, France, Ireland, the Netherlands, Norway, Poland, Portugal, Spain, and other countries in Europe have been accurately considered nation-states. For much of the past century, Italy and Germany have been united as nation-states, too.

In other cases, it is less clear that a country is actually a nation-state. This is true in the case of Great Britain, which is actually made up of the English, the Scotch, the Welsh, and some of the Irish. The same is also true for Belgium, which has large percentages of Fleming and Walloon, many of whom consider themselves to be Flemish or Walloon, not Belgian. Switzerland presents a similar case. Most Swiss are ethnically German, French, or Italian, but most nevertheless consider themselves Swiss. However, some view themselves as Germans, French, or Italian.

In still other cases, it is exceedingly clear that a country that once was called a nation-state is not a nation-state. For years, Czechoslovakia, the Soviet Union, and Yugoslavia were called nations or nation-states. However, it has become clear that these were states that consisted of several nations. They were not true nation-states. All three have been torn apart by national groups that demanded their own nation-states.

What about the United States? In the traditional sense, the United States – and other states that have large percentages of more than one nationality living within them – are not nation-states. Nevertheless, few would deny that a "U.S. nationalism" exists. But it is not a narrowly-defined, ethnically-based nationalism. At least in theory, U.S. nationalism is multi-ethnic and inclusive. U.S. nationalism links American to American because of the ideals and values which the U.S. espouses. Nevertheless, even though U.S. nationalism is value-driven rather than ethnically driven, most U.S. citizens exhibit "nationalism" about the United States, feel linked to other Americans, and express pride about their country.

Modern European Nationalism

Where did nationalism in Europe come from, and what role does it play in Europe today? As a concept, nationalism is several centuries old. But when the state first emerged in Europe in the seventeenth century as a way to organize society, nationalism was only rarely associated with a state. Rather, citizens of a state pledged allegiance to the individual who ruled the state. "L'etat, c'est moi" ("The state, it is I"), said King Louis XIV of France, and he was right.

This situation remained in place in most of Europe until the end of the eighteenth century. Gradually, people who lived in certain states came to believe that the state belonged to them as much as to the monarch. Thus, as people who lived in a state began to identify more and more with each other instead of with the monarch, modern nationalism and the modern nation-state were born.

Nationalism in Europe and elsewhere as well may be expressed in many ways. Depending on how it is expressed, nationalism may range from the one extreme of being constructive and helpful to the other extreme of being destructive and dangerous.

Positive manifestations of nationalism include efforts to raise standards of living, attempts to win more gold medals than others at the Olympics, and depending on how it is carried out, the desire of members of a nation to control and govern the territory in which they live.

Unfortunately, there is also another side to nationalism. In its more extreme form, nationalism does more than psychologically bind together people who identify with one another, instill them with pride in whom and what they are, and lead them to seek self-rule. In its extreme form, nationalism may also lead one nation to ascribe superiority to itself over others, and to create a desire in one nation to control and exploit other nations, their territories, and their wealth.

Along with economics, this extreme form of nationalism was one of the main driving forces behind European colonial expansion during the eighteenth, nineteenth, and early twentieth centuries. It also contributed significantly to the national rivalries that led to World War I, and to German territorial expansion that led to World War II.

Sometimes, it is difficult to gauge when nationalism is constructive and helpful, or when it is dangerous and even destructive. The cases of the European Union, the dissolution of Czechoslovakia, and the anti-foreign sentiment that swept many European states in the early 1990s provide excellent examples of the positive and negative dimensions of nationalism.

In the case of the European Union, as we have already seen, many Europeans fear that the drive for greater integration and eventual unity will lead to the loss of national identity, national culture, and national self-determination. It is not clear whether or not their fears are warranted.

However, even if their fears are justified, another question must be asked. Would the advantages that might be derived from greater European integration and eventual unity – for example, fewer wars in Europe and a greater economic growth rate – be sufficient to offset the possible loss of national identity, culture, and self-determination? No one knows for sure, but everyone has an opinion.

Similarly, in Czechoslovakia, was it for the Czech and Slovak peoples to be united in a single state, Czechoslovakia, as was the case for most of the period between 1918 and 1993? Or will it be better for the Czechs and Slovaks (and for all of Europe), that each now has its own country, the Czech Republic and Slovakia? Only time will tell.

More frightening was the wave of anti-foreign sentiment that swept France, Germany, Great Britain, and other European states in the early 1990s. In all cases, nationalist animosity was directed against foreigners because foreigners had different values, different cultures, or took jobs that nationalists claimed could have gone to citizens of their own country.

Many people dismissed the wave of anti-foreign sentiment, some of which led to murder, as insignificant, representing only a small minority of European public sentiment. Other observers warned of a drift toward neo-Nazism.

Who was right? Again, no one knew. But in at least one case in Europe, it was clear that nationalism could be unarguably dangerous and destructive. That case was the former Yugoslavia.

Yugoslavia

Yugoslavia was created in 1918 by the Treaty of Versailles that ended World War I. It included territory taken from the old Austro-Hungarian Empire, which collapsed during World War I, and all the territory of Serbia and Montenegro, two states that had been independent since 1878 after they broke free from the old Ottoman Empire, which also collapsed during World War I.

Yugoslavia brought many nationalities together within one state and under one government. The predominant nationalities were Croats, Serbs, and Slovenes. Indeed, Yugoslavia's original name was the Kingdom of the Serbs, Croats, and Slovenes. In addition, large numbers of Muslim Slavs lived in Yugoslavia, especially in Bosnia-Herzegovina, one of the regions that had been added to Yugoslavia from Austria-Hungary.

Between World Wars I and II, Yugoslavia struggled with internal rivalries between its several nationalities. The primary dispute was between the Serbs and Croats. After the leader of the Croat Peasant Party was shot on the floor of the National Assembly in 1928, King Alexander I dissolved parliament and took over the government himself. In an effort to promote national unity, he also at this time changed the name of his kingdom to Yugoslavia.

Germany invaded Yugoslavia in 1941. It established a puppet Croatian government called the "Ustache" in the Croatia and Bosnia-Herzegovina portions of Yugoslavia. The Ustache killed as many as 400,000 Serbs during its three-year rule. Serbs retaliated against Croatians, but on a much smaller scale. Many of the Serb fighters, called Chetniks, were Royalists who sought the return of the Yugoslav monarchy.

After Germany invaded the Soviet Union in June 1941, the Yugoslav Communist Party, under the leadership of Josef Tito, also became a major player in the unfolding Yugoslav drama. Tito's forces slowly gathered strength, and with limited aid from the Soviet Army, Tito forced Germany out of Yugoslavia in 1944.

The war had been a horrible experience for Yugoslavia. The country suffered immense destruction. Even worse, Yugoslavs had been brutal to each other. Yugoslavs killed at least one million other Yugoslavs during the war years.

Following World War II, Tito and his communists assumed power in Yugoslavia. In 1948, Tito's regime became the first communist government to reject Moscow's directions. Tito found this substantially easier to do than did other communist leaders because Tito had attained power with little Soviet help.

Tito, like King Alexander I before him, struggled to create a Yugoslav nationalism. Despite the political, ethnic, economic, and social strains that existed in Yugoslavia, it appeared for a time that he might succeed.

However, demands by Yugoslavia's separate nationalities led Yugoslavia in 1974 to adopt a new constitution that shifted power from the central government in Belgrade to the six republics and two autonomous regions that made up the country. As region began to compete with region, the entire Yugoslavian economy suffered.

Then, in 1980, Tito, the primary advocate of Yugoslavian nationalism and unity, died. Following his death, a rotating presidency was created that passed between the leaders of each republic. Meanwhile, political and economic reform movements grew in several regions, moving those regions further away from the diluted form of communism advocated by the central government.

In 1987, Slobodan Milosevic, an ardent Serb nationalist and avid communist, became Serbia's leader. He soon began to appeal to Serbian national pride in an effort to keep Yugoslavia together and to end what he called the oppression of Serbs living in other Yugoslav republics.

Non-Serbian Yugoslavs saw Milosevic's positions as ethnic, political, and ideological threats. As a result, the already-existing trend toward Yugoslavian dissolution accelerated.

Slovenia was the first republic to gain independence. In April 1990, a non-communist party, DEMOS, won Slovenia's elections. In July 1990, the Slovene National Assembly declared that Yugoslavian laws only applied to Slovenia when they did not contradict Slovenian laws. In December 1990, an overwhelming majority of Slovenes voted for an "independent and sovereign state." On June 25, 1991, Slovenia declared independence.

A brief war followed in which the Belgrade government made a halfhearted attempt to prevent Slovenia's secession. But on July 18, Belgrade withdrew its forces from Slovenia. From the Belgrade government's perspective, Slovenia was relatively unimportant, at least in comparison to Croatia, which was also moving rapidly toward independence. In addition, many more Serbs lived in Croatia than in Slovenia.

Events in Croatia paralleled those in Slovenia. In April 1990, a non-communist Croat nationalist party, HDZ, won the election. In May 1991, Croatians voted overwhelmingly for independence, and on June 25, Croatia declared independence.

Many Serbs living in Croatia remembered the Croatian Ustache of World War II, and were terrified. This, in combination with Serbian nationalism, led some to argue that they should secede from Croatia and join what was left of Yugoslavia, thereby creating a "Greater Serbia."

These actions and reactions led to ethnic fighting throughout Croatia in late 1990 and throughout 1991. Often, it was quite violent. Efforts by the EC, the UN, and individual states to end the fighting in Croatia accomplished little. Even the recognition of Croatia by the EC and the United States and the deployment of 14,000 UN peacekeeping troops to Croatia quieted the fighting only temporarily. By 1993, warfare in Croatia continued.

As violent as the Croatian conflict was, it paled in comparison to the war in Bosnia-Herzegovina. Geographically, Bosnia-Herzegovina is between Serbia and Croatia.

Ethnically, Bosnia-Herzegovina was the most diverse of all Yugoslav republics. Seventeen percent of its population was Croat, 32 percent Serb, and 42 percent Muslim Slavic.

Given its location and its ethnic composition, Bosnia-Herzegovina was doomed to be the scene of bloody fighting. But few people expected the fighting to be as bloody or brutal as it was. Most analysts and observers agreed that Serbs living in Bosnia-Herzegovina, aided and abetted by Serbia itself, were the most brutal combatants, indiscriminately attacking cities and villages, using rape as a weapon of war, and pursuing a policy of "ethnic cleansing" that sought to drive Muslims out of Bosnia-Herzegovina. But all sides participated in the murder that took place there.

By early 1994, over 100,000 people had been killed in Bosnia-Herzegovina. Perhaps a million more had fled Bosnia-Herzegovina and become refugees. Meanwhile, the international community, deep in debate over what to do, did virtually nothing except provide limited humanitarian assistance.

What was the right course of action to end the killing, most of which was caused by ethnic animosity and nationalism gone berserk? What did the breakup of Yugoslavia and the death and destruction there portend for other states in Europe and elsewhere that included multiple ethnic groups? Were the atrocities in Bosnia-Herzegovina one last spasm of ethnic and nationalist violence in a century of nationalism-induced violence that was drawing to a close? Or were the atrocities only the first spasm of a new wave of nationalism-induced violence of a century about to begin? No one knew.

Issues for the U.S. and the World

Nationalism has long been an important force in European affairs. As we see in Europe today, it is an extremely emotional issue that is difficult to address objectively. In the SCIS videotape, "Europe After the Cold War," Lesson 3, "Nationalism in Europe," the former Secretaries of State engage in a detailed discussion of nationalism, and what, if anything, the U.S. should do about the situation in the former Yugoslavia. They examine several important issues such as:

1. **the positive and negative impacts of nationalism.** What are the root causes of nationalism? What are some of the positive and negative effects of nationalism that can be seen in Europe today? Why are some countries able to absorb diverse ethnic groups, and others not? Why in some cases does nationalism lead to armed conflict? What can countries do to counter the destructive side of nationalism?

2. **the United States and Yugoslavia.** The former Secretaries debate whether the United States could have and should have acted to prevent the dissolution of Yugoslavia and the ensuing fighting there. A key issue of discussion is whether the United States should have acted militarily. What is the range of options that they present? Which perspective do you support? Why?

3. **governing a country with diverse nationalities.** Secretary Shultz points out that governing a country that has diverse nationalities is a difficult task. The U.S. has met this challenge reasonably well, but other states, such as

Czechoslovakia and Yugoslavia, have failed. Why does nationalism lead to civil wars in some cases but not others? Do you agree with Secretary Rogers, who asserts that it is almost impossible to expect diverse national groups to live together? Why?

4. **nationalism and immigration.** Secretary Rogers observes that the reason that Germany is experiencing a surge of nationalism is because of the flow of immigrants into Germany. He implies that the EC policy of open borders will lead to the growth of nationalist feelings, not only in Germany, but in other EC member states as well. Do you agree with his analysis? Why or why not?

Selected Bibliography

Anderson, Benedict. Imagined Communities: Reflections on the Origin and Spread of Nationalism (New York: Routledge, 1991).

Brown, J.F. Nationalism, Democracy, and Security in the Balkans (Brookfield, VT: Dartmouth Publishing Company, 1992).

Cohen, Lenard J. Broken Bonds: The Disintegration of Yugoslavia (Boulder, CO: Westview, 1993).

Connor, Walker. Ethnonationalism: The Quest for Understanding (Princeton, NJ: Princeton University Press, 1994).

Dragnich, Alex N. Serbs and Croats: The Struggle in Yugoslavia (New York: Harcourt, Brace, Jovanovich, 1992).

Griffiths, Stephen Iwan. Nationalism in Central and Eastern Europe: A Threat to European Security? (New York: Oxford University Press, 1993).

Kedourie, Elie. Nationalism (Cambridge, MA: Blackwell, 1993).

LESSON 3

NATIONALISM IN EUROPE

Activity 1:

WHAT IS A STATE, NATION, AND NATION-STATE?

ACTIVITY OBJECTIVE

The student will be able to define the terms state, nation, nation-state, and nationalism, and understand what they mean.

MATERIALS AND RESOURCES

❑ Teacher Resource 3.1 "Definitions of State, Nation, and Nation-State"

❑ Current almanacs

❑ Index cards

STRATEGIES

Begin the lesson by asking students to define nationalism. Many textbooks use a definition such as "A feeling of loyalty to one's own land and people." Explain that this lesson will help students have a clearer understanding of the depth of the term "nationalism." Make a transparency from Teacher Resource 3.1 (or distribute it as a handout). Have students read and discuss the definitions. Explain that other sources may give different definitions. After this activity, students may want to create their own definitions.

Write the following names of countries or groups on index cards or small pieces of paper. Make a set of cards for each group. Each set should contain a minimum of 8 cards. Cards should include: **France, Norway, Flanders, Spain, Germany, Ireland, Italy, Scotland, United Kingdom, Greece, Czechoslovakia, Europe, Switzerland, Russia, Lithuania, Bosnia and the United States.** Divide students into small groups and give each group a set of the cards. Have the students divide the cards into the following categories: **State, Nation-State**, and **Nation.** If needed provide each group with a current almanac which will help them to determine the number of ethnic/linguistic/religious populations in each country. Write on the board **State, Nation-State, and Nation.** Choose students to come to the board and tape a card in the appropriate category. The student should be able to defend the placement. Allow time for other students to dispute the placement. Place the card in the category where MOST students believe it should be. Cards may also overlap categories. Continue this activity until all of the cards have been categorized.

Note: There could develop among the groups a little frustration in trying to categorize all the terms. This should be anticipated. Explain to students that it may be impossible to come to consensus on the placement of some countries. (See the Study Guide for Lesson 3 for help in determining placement of the cards.)

Provide closure by asking questions such as:

- Based on the growing ethnic diversity in the United States, would our country best fit the definition of "state" or "nation-state"?

- What role does outside recognition play in adding legitimacy to the claim of being a "nation-state"? (e.g., Lithuania is generally recognized by the world community as a nation-state. How might this apply to other areas of the world?)

Finally, review the definitions of state, nation, nation-state, and nationalism as they apply to the changing world order.

DEFINITIONS OF STATE, NATION, AND NATION-STATE

Until recently, the term "nation" was used almost interchangeably with "state" and "nation-state." It was never correct to do this, but nevertheless, it was widely done. This is changing. The break-up of Czechoslovakia, the Soviet Union, and Yugoslavia, and the nationality difficulties that Belgium, Canada, Great Britain, India and other states throughout the world are having, make it extremely important that the differences between the three terms are understood.

A **state** is an area of the earth's surface that has human-created boundaries. A state is governed by a central authority that makes laws, rules, and decisions that it enforces within those boundaries. A state makes its own policies, and the government of a state recognizes no earthly authority higher than itself within its own boundaries.

A **nation** need not necessarily control an area of the earth's surface, nor have a government or make policy. A nation is simply a group of people who view themselves as being linked to one another in some manner. Groups of people who consider themselves to be ethnically, culturally, or linguistically related may thus be considered a nation. In essence, a nation is a psychological fixation as much as anything else.

A **nation-state** is a state whose inhabitants consider themselves to be a nation. It is an area of the earth's surface with human-created boundaries under a single government, the population of which considers itself to be in some way, shape, or form, related.

Nationalism is closely related to the concepts of nation and nation-state. In simplest terms, nationalism is the psychological force that binds people together who identify with each other. Nationalism refers to the feelings of attachment that members of a nation have to one another, and to their nation-state.

LESSON 3

NATIONALISM IN EUROPE

Activity 2:

WHAT ARE SOME POSITIVE AND NEGATIVE EXAMPLES OF NATIONALISM?

ACTIVITY OBJECTIVE

The student will be able to identify concrete positive and negative examples of nationalism in real world situations.

MATERIALS AND RESOURCES

❏ SCIS Videotape "Europe After the Cold War," Lesson 3, "Nationalism in Europe"
❏ Worksheet 3.1 "Positive and Negative Examples of Nationalism"
❏ U.S. and world history textbooks
❏ Current newspapers and news magazines

STRATEGIES

Nationalism can be either a positive or negative force depending on the circumstances. For example, during the Olympics, nationalism encourages athletes to work hard in order to win gold medals for their country. In the 1960s, nationalism pushed the United States into the exploration of space. However, nationalism can also be a very negative force when in extreme cases it leads one nation to consider itself superior to another.

Divide students into groups of four. Distribute Worksheet 3.1 "Positive and Negative Examples of Nationalism." Show students the SCIS Videotape "Europe After the Cold War," Lesson 3, "Nationalism in Europe," and instruct students to enter examples of nationalism that are discussed on the videotape into the appropriate category.

Next, assign each group to find additional examples of one of the categories. For students researching historical examples, provide U.S. and world history textbooks. For students researching current examples, provide newspapers and news magazines. (See Study Guide Lesson 3 for additional examples of the positive and negative influences of nationalism.)   Have students share their examples within the group and then allow time for each group to share with the class.

Ask students to draw some conclusions about the role of nationalism both in the past and in the present. For example, one difference that seems to be developing is that during World Wars I and II, nationalism led nation-states to conquer additional territories. Today, nationalism appears to be more directed at dividing states into their constituent elements, as in Yugoslavia, Czechoslovakia, and the Soviet Union.

POSITIVE AND NEGATIVE EXAMPLES
OF NATIONALISM

POSITIVE EXAMPLES FROM HISTORY	POSITIVE EXAMPLES FROM PRESENT
NEGATIVE EXAMPLES FROM HISTORY	NEGATIVE EXAMPLES FROM PRESENT

LESSON 3

NATIONALISM IN EUROPE

Activity 3:

HOW HAS HISTORY IMPACTED THE CURRENT SITUATION IN THE BALKANS?

ACTIVITY OBJECTIVE

The student will understand the background to the warfare that broke out in the former Yugoslavia in the 1990s.

MATERIALS AND RESOURCES

❑ Handout 3.1 "The Division of the Balkans"

❑ Handout 3.2 "The Formation and Dissolution of Yugoslavia"

❑ Current news articles, editorials, and cartoons about the Balkans

STRATEGIES

Distribute to small groups (in a manila folder, if possible) Handout 3.1, "The Division of Yugoslavia," and Handout 3.2, "The Formation and Dissolution of Yugoslavia." Also include in the folder other current news articles, editorials, and/or cartoons concerning the current status of the Balkans. Place enough articles in each folder so that each group member has at least two articles/cartoons to read and interpret. Have the group leader distribute the materials equally among the group. Each student should read and study his/her article or handout and write down the key concepts. The key concepts of all of the articles should be shared with the group. While monitoring the group work, determine if students understand the information in Handouts 3.1 and 3.2. If misunderstandings arise, the teacher may need to provide additional explanation.

Read the following directions to the students. Write questions A and B on the board.

> Answer the following questions as a group. The recorder should write the answers. Out in the margin indicate the name of the person who contributed the different parts to the answers. Each answer should be at least one page.
>
> > A. What is the current situation in the Balkans?
> > B. How has history affected the current situation?

Once each group has answered the questions, have it share its answers with the class. Make sure students understand the significance of the Battle of Kosovo (1389), the Pan-Slavism movement before World War I and the role of the Roman Catholic, Eastern Orthodox, and Islamic faiths in the region. Next, have each group draw a political cartoon which depicts the current situation in the Balkans. The cartoon should show evidence of understanding the history of the region and the current situation. Display students' cartoons when they are finished.

DIVISION OF THE BALKANS

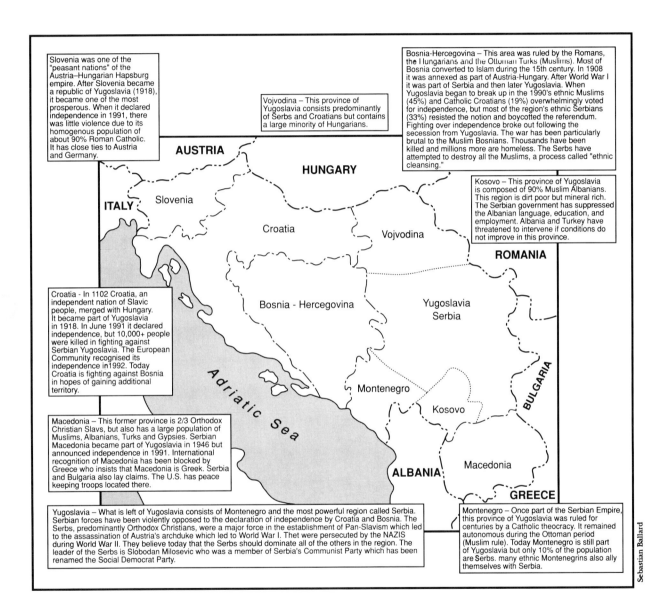

Slovenia was one of the "peasant nations" of the Austria–Hungarian Hapsburg empire. After Slovenia became a republic of Yugoslavia (1918), it became one of the most prosperous. When it declared independence in 1991, there was little violence due to its homogenous population of about 90% Roman Catholic. It has close ties to Austria and Germany.

Vojvodina – This province of Yugoslavia consists predominantly of Serbs and Croatians but contains a large minority of Hungarians.

Bosnia-Hercegovina – This area was ruled by the Romans, the Hungarians and the Ottoman Turks (Muslims). Most of Bosnia converted to Islam during the 15th century. In 1908 it was annexed as part of Austria-Hungary. After World War I it was part of Serbia and then later Yugoslavia. When Yugoslavia began to break up in the 1990's ethnic Muslims (45%) and Catholic Croatians (19%) overwhelmingly voted for independence, but most of the region's ethnic Serbians (33%) resisted the notion and boycotted the referendum. Fighting over independence broke out following the secession from Yugoslavia. The war has been particularly brutal to the Muslim Bosnians. Thousands have been killed and millions more are homeless. The Serbs have attempted to destroy all the Muslims, a process called "ethnic cleansing."

Kosovo – This province of Yugoslavia is composed of 90% Muslim Albanians. This region is dirt poor but mineral rich. The Serbian government has suppressed the Albanian language, education, and employment. Albania and Turkey have threatened to intervene if conditions do not improve in this province.

Croatia - In 1102 Croatia, an independent nation of Slavic people, merged with Hungary. It became part of Yugoslavia in 1918. In June 1991 it declared independence, but 10,000+ people were killed in fighting against Serbian Yugoslavia. The European Community recognised its independence in1992. Today Croatia is fighting against Bosnia in hopes of gaining additional territory.

Macedonia – This former province is 2/3 Orthodox Christian Slavs, but also has a large population of Muslims, Albanians, Turks and Gypsies. Serbian Macedonia became part of Yugoslavia in 1946 but announced independence in 1991. International recognition of Macedonia has been blocked by Greece who insists that Macedonia is Greek. Serbia and Bulgaria also lay claims. The U.S. has peace keeping troops located there.

Yugoslavia – What is left of Yugoslavia consists of Montenegro and the most powerful region called Serbia. Serbian forces have been violently opposed to the declaration of independence by Croatia and Bosnia. The Serbs, predominantly Orthodox Christians, were a major force in the establishment of Pan-Slavism which led to the assassination of Austria's archduke which led to World War I. Thet were persecuted by the NAZIS during World War II. They believe today that the Serbs should dominate all of the others in the region. The leader of the Serbs is Slobodan Milosevic who was a member of Serbia's Communist Party which has been renamed the Social Democrat Party.

Montenegro – Once part of the Serbian Empire, this province of Yugoslavia was ruled for centuries by a Catholic theocracy. It remained autonomous during the Ottoman period (Muslim rule). Today Montenegro is still part of Yugoslavia but only 10% of the population are Serbs. many ethnic Montenegrins also ally themselves with Serbia.

Map labels: AUSTRIA, HUNGARY, ITALY, Slovenia, Croatia, Vojvodina, ROMANIA, Bosnia - Hercegovina, Yugoslavia Serbia, Adriatic Sea, Montenegro, Kosovo, BULGARIA, Macedonia, ALBANIA, GREECE

Sebastian Ballard

THE FORMATION AND DISSOLUTION OF YUGOSLAVIA

A.D.

395   Roman Empire splits into Eastern and Western parts; Serbs are Eastern Orthodox and Croatians are Roman Catholic.

952-1102   Croatia is an independent Kingdom.

1102   Croatia loses independence to Hungary.

1331-55   "Golden Age" of Medieval Serbia.

1389   Ottoman Turks (Muslims) crush Serbia at the Battle of Kosovo; begin 500 years of repressive Ottoman rule. Bosnia and Herzegovina provide the largest number of converts to Islam. Their descendants are today's Bosnian Muslims. During Ottoman rule, the Eastern Orthodox Serbs were barred from politics and trade and were heavily taxed.

1699   Roman Catholic Croats came under control of the Catholic-controlled Austro-Hungarian Empire (Slovenia was already a part of Austria-Hungary).

1718-1878 Turks are slowly pushed out of Croatia and Serbia.

1878   European Treaty gives freedom to Serbia; gives Bosnia to Austria-Hungary.

1912-13   Balkan Wars; Serbia tries to create a "Greater Serbia" which would include predominantly Slavic peoples of the Balkans, including Bosnia.

1914   Assassination of Austria-Hungary's archduke Franz Ferdinand (in the province of Bosnia); Austria declares war on Serbia (assassins were members of the Black Hand, but were also from Serbia); Russia, France and Britain come to the aid of Serbia against the Central Powers of Germany and Austria-Hungary.

1918   A new Kingdom comes from the treaties at Versailles; unites Slavs.

1929   The name Yugoslavia – Land of the Southern Slavs – is adopted.

1941   Nazis occupy Yugoslavia; partisans battle the Germans and each other; Croatian allies of the Nazis try to exterminate the Serbs.

1945   Communist leader Josip Broz Tito takes power.

1948   Yugoslavia leaves the Soviet bloc; remains communist.

1965   Economic reforms gradually loosen central control from Belgrade.

1974   New constitution further weakens central control from Belgrade.

1980   Tito dies. Strong controlling power is gone from Yugoslavia.

1988   Nationalist movements begin in Serbia, Croatia, Slovenia (republics of Yugoslavia).

1990   Communist Party falls in Croatia and Slovenia.

1991   Slovenia, Bosnia, Macedonia secede from Yugoslavia; war in Croatia.

1992   War erupts in Bosnia; U.N. recognizes Croatia and Slovenia.

1993   Numerous cease-fires between Bosnia and Serbia (major province in Yugoslavia) fail. Croatia fights against Bosnia in hopes of gaining additional territory.

LESSON 3

NATIONALISM IN EUROPE

Activity 4:

WHAT ROLE SHOULD THE U.S. PLAY IN THE BALKANS?

ACTIVITY OBJECTIVES

The student will understand the complexities of the policy choices that the United States faced in the Balkans situation of 1993.

MATERIALS AND RESOURCES

❑   Worksheet 3.2 "Quotes from the Former Secretaries of State"

❑   SCIS Videotape "Europe After the Cold War," Lesson 3, "Nationalism in Europe"

STRATEGIES

Distribute to the class Worksheet 3.2, "Quotes from the Former Secretaries of State." Have students watch the SCIS Videotape, "Europe after the Cold War," Lesson 3, "Nationalism in Europe." As they watch the videotape, have students identify the person who is the source of each of the quotes. After they have matched the quote to the correct secretary, have the students give a short explanation of each of the quotes in the space provided on the worksheet. Allow students to share the explanations with a partner.

Choose three students in the class to role-play each of the secretaries quoted in the tape (William Rogers, Alexander Haig, and George Shultz). Allow some time for students to look over all of the quotes from the person they are to role-play to determine their position on the situation in Yugoslavia. Then ask the three students to come to the front of the room and respond to the following question in the way they BELIEVE their secretary would respond:

What role should the United States play in the current situation in the Balkans?

The rest of the class should judge whether the students' answers seem to be appropriate or not. Remind students that this was taped in February 1993. Situations could change so that any of these men might alter the position stated at that time.

Students may complete the activity by writing a pro or con editorial stating their opinions of the U.S. role in the Balkans.

QUOTES FROM THE FORMER SECRETARIES OF STATE

As you watch Lesson 3 of the SCIS Videotape "Europe After the Cold War," identify the person who made each of the following quotes. They are all former Secretaries of State and the quotes come from their meeting in Little Rock, Arkansas in January 1993. After you have watched the tape, give a brief explanation of the quote.

I. "The real question is do we get involved militarily [in Bosnia]. My own view is I don't think we should now."

Source:

Explanation:

II. "We must be advocates of rule of law and peaceful change and due process. And if in the process of bringing ethnic purity to the fore there is violation of law, we must oppose it. If it happens through peaceful means and negotiation, then we can endorse it.... In this instance there is violation of law on the part of the Serbian leaders, and as a world community we must oppose it."

Source:

Explanation:

III. "There is no way I think that you can stand around and say mediate when an agreement is announced and at the same time Sarajevo is being shelled. And we have incontrovertible evidence of all sorts of violations of people, of systematic rape of young girls [and] of all sorts of terrible things. We have a situation where all of the arms are in the hands of one party and not in the other. So we have an embargo that tells the forces that might want to defend themselves — that do defend themselves — that they can't get any arms. I saw a man who was a world-class soccer player going back to his home in Yugoslavia. [When he] was asked why he did that, he said, "A man who won't defend his home doesn't deserve to have one."

Source:

Explanation:

IV. "We have gone to the United Nations and pointed up these human rights matters which are terrible. We now in retrospect say [of] the Holocaust, how terrible that was. And how just as terrible it was that somehow it happened and nobody paid any attention. Nobody did anything about it. Well, we have exactly the same thing. What is ethnic cleansing?"

Source:

Explanation:

V. "I don't know what we'd do if we got in Yugoslavia. Shoot down a few airplanes? Certainly that's a start, but where do you stop when that continues?"

Source:

Explanation:

VI. "Anyone who's against doing anything [and] would rather negotiate any problem is going to take that line."

Source:

Explanation:

VII "The most difficult problem of governance is how you govern over diversity of various kinds.... And so you have to learn to govern over it [and] how to so arrange things that people can honor their varying roots but at the same time have an overall common purpose that allows them to live together successfully."

Source:

Explanation:

VIII. "I think that the use of force to try to... I'm talking about military force now... to make other people do what we think they should do is fruitless and dangerous."

Source:

Explanation:

IX. **"I think we have in this world, and this is an important issue . . . a transparency that's come out of globalism which now makes it impossible for heads of state and government to ignore atrocities, injustices, and conflict in the world."**

Source:

Explanation:

LESSON 4

THE GERMAN QUESTION

Lesson 4 of 6 Lesson Plans for the
Southern Center for International Studies'
High School Educational Package
EUROPE AFTER THE COLD WAR

The opening of the Berlin Wall in November 1989 led to the unification of East and West Germany in October 1990, ending 45 years of division.

LESSON 4
of the SCIS Educational Package
EUROPE AFTER THE COLD WAR

THE GERMAN QUESTION

The end of the Cold War, the drive toward European integration and unification, and the reemergence of ethnic nationalism within Europe all had immense importance for another issue central to the future of Europe, the German question.

The core of the German question can be easily phrased: "What is Germany, what might Germany become, and what does this mean for Europe and the world?" The answer to the question is more difficult.

The German Question: Where It Came From

Until the late nineteenth century, there was no single Germany. Rather, Germans lived in a number of separate duchies, city-states, states, kingdoms, and empires. Situated in the heart of Europe, and inhabited by hard-working, cultured, educated, and ambitious people, these duchies, city-states, states, kingdoms, and empires never combined into a single state as had occurred in much of the rest of Europe. Indeed, without easily defensible boundaries, the territory inhabited by Germans was often invaded and controlled by others, including the French, the Swedes, and the Poles.

This began to change in the mid-nineteenth century. By then, Prussia was widely recognized as the most important and powerful German state. After Prussia defeated France in the 1870 Franco-Prussian War, several German states united under Prussian leadership, and the German Empire was formed. At about the same time, industrialization accelerated throughout much of what had become Germany.

Between 1870 and 1914, Germany became one of the major players on the European scene. Like other European states, it sought to enhance its economic strength, political power, and military capabilities on the European continent and beyond. By 1914, Germany, France, and Great Britain were widely recognized as the leading powers in the world.

Germany's efforts to expand its economic, political, and military capabilities added to the already-existing rivalries for power, prestige, and position that existed among European states. Together, these rivalries were among the several primary causes of World War I. Germany's defeat in that war led to the Versailles Peace Treaty, a punative peace under which the victorious powers, especially France and Great Britain, sought to punish Germany.

To optimists of the day, the Versailles Treaty answered the German question. The treaty demilitarized Germany, stripped it of much of its industry, and transferred the province of Alsace-Lorraine from Germany back to France. Pessimists feared that the Versailles Treaty had not answered the German question, but had undermined the possibility of German economic stability, and added fuel to German desires for revenge.

The pessimists were right. The German economy floundered, German resentment grew, and a political crisis within Germany influenced German president Hindenburg to appoint Adolph Hitler chancellor. With their leader as chancellor, the Nazis soon seized power. Germany built up its industrial and military might under Hitler and the Nazis during the early and middle 1930s, and used that might to create a German-controlled "Fortress Europe" during the late 1930s and early 1940s.

Germany's World War II defeat again brought the German question to the forefront of European affairs. This time, however, most of Europe was in ruins. Thus, two non-European powers, the United States and the Soviet Union, had the greatest role in trying to answer the German question: "What is Germany, what might Germany become, and what does this mean for Europe and the world?"

Germany in the Cold War

At the Yalta Conference just before the end of World War II, the United States, the Soviet Union, and Great Britain agreed that they, along with France, should split Germany into four zones of occupation. The occupying country would have the responsibility of administering all affairs within its zone of occupation. Each occupying power was free to decide how to administer its own zone. Berlin, Germany's capital situated deep within the Soviet occupation zone, would also be divided into four parts. It was also agreed that all four zones of Germany and Berlin would eventually be unified. Until then, all major decisions affecting Germany were to be made by the four-power "Allied Control Commission," located in Berlin.

Two major issues relating to Germany soon separated the World War II allies. The first was Germany's future political orientation. In the Western zones, Western-style political and economic reforms were actively encouraged. Conversely, in the Soviet zone, the U.S.S.R., acting in conjunction with German communists, aided the growth of communist power and control. Soviet actions and statements also made it evident that the U.S.S.R. intended to establish extensive influence throughout Germany once unification occurred.

Given the general deterioration of East-West relations in late 1945 and 1946 as a result of Soviet actions in Eastern Europe, Iran, and Turkey, the Western Allies could not accept the growth of Soviet influence. In addition, the Western allies' intention was to create a democratic pro-Western Germany, not a communist pro-Soviet Germany. A deadlock was therefore quickly reached about Germany's political future.

The second issue was economics. At the February 1945 Yalta Conference, the U.S., the U.S.S.R., and Great Britain reached agreement on $20 billion as a figure for discussion for reparations for the U.S.S.R. It was also suggested that reparations might be taken from Germany as a whole.

But by July 1945, when the Potsdam Conference was held, the situation had changed. The new U.S. President, Harry Truman, refused to set any specific figure for reparations, pointing out that the $20 billion was only a figure for discussion. He also suggested that reparations be taken by each country from their respective zones of occupation, not from Germany as a whole. The Soviets objected to both points, arguing that $20 billion was the reparation figure that had been agreed to, and that if reparations were taken from zones of occupation rather than Germany as a whole, the U.S.S.R could not obtain reparations from Germany's industrially-rich Ruhr Valley. Deadlock over economic issues therefore followed as well.

With agreement about the political and economic future of Germany nowhere in sight, and with East-West tension growing throughout Europe and the world, no peace conference was held to end World War II. Recognizing that a peace conference was not probable and that German unification from their perspective was neither likely nor desirable given Soviet objectives, the U.S. and Great Britain in 1947 moved to unite their zones of occupation, creating "Bizonia." Soon thereafter, the French zone was added to Bizonia, and "Trizonia" came into being.

The Soviets objected to the gradual unification of the three Western occupation zones, and applied subtle and not so subtle pressures to show their displeasure. For example, in January 1948, the U.S.S.R. both stopped coal deliveries from its occupation zone into West Berlin and refused to permit West Berliners to travel freely to the western occupation zones of Germany. At the same time, in their own occupation zone, they proceeded to establish a communist government and society. The Western powers, in turn, protested to the Soviets.

The final split between East and West over the German question came in June 1948 when the three Western powers instituted a currency reform in Trizonia to accelerate its economic recovery. The Soviets responded to this Western "provocation" by blockading all land access routes to Berlin. For eleven months, U.S., British, and French forces supplied all of Berlin's needs via air. The Berlin Blockade and the ensuing Berlin Airlift thus marked the true break-point between East and West over the German question.

For the next forty-five years, Germany was divided. Throughout that period, the two parts of Germany developed different political, economic, and social systems. In East Germany (the German Democratic Republic), the Soviets, in conjunction with East German communists, instituted a centralized communist political, economic, and social system. On one occasion, in 1953, the Soviets suppressed anti-communist demonstrations in East Germany. Neverthless, the Soviet presence remained, and communization proceeded. East Germany became the most loyal of all Eastern European Soviet allies.

Meanwhile, in West Germany (the Federal Republic of Germany), the Western Allies and West Germans developed a decentralized, multi-party democratic political system; a free-market economic system; and a decentralized, liberal social system. Integrated fully into the Western alliance, West Germany became a true success story.

On several occasions during East and West Germany's forty-five years of separation, disagreements between the U.S. and the Soviet Union over Berlin threatened to erupt into war. In all cases, the crises were precipitated by the U.S.S.R. In addition to the 1948 Berlin blockade, other notable Berlin crises occurred in 1958 when Soviet leader Nikita Khrushchev threatened to sign a separate peace treaty with East Germany and turn all access routes to Berlin over to the East German government, and in 1961 when the Soviets and East Germans built the Berlin Wall.

Between 1945 and 1969, it remained official West German and Western policy to seek the unification of Germany. However, the reality of the situation was that no one expected unification.

Then, in 1969, the Social Democrats won control of the West German Parliament for the first time, defeating the Christian Democrats. They immediately renounced the goal of unifying East and West Germany, saying instead that they sought to achieve reconciliation between the two. This meant that the two Germany would now coexist. With this, the way was clear to reduce East-West tensions over Germany.

Thus, in August 1970, West Germany and the Soviet Union concluded an agreement in which both renounced the use of force and recognized the existing borders of all states in Europe. Four months later, West Germany and Poland signed a similar treaty. Then, in September 1972, the four countries that occupied Germany at the end of World War II — France, Great Britain, the Soviet Union, and the United States — reached agreement on the status of Berlin. The West conceded that West Berlin was not a "constituent element" of West Germany, and in return received guaranteed access to the city and Soviet accession to the right to develop cultural and other ties between West Germany and West Berlin. Next, after only four months of negotiations, East and West Germany in December 1972 concluded an accord that amounted to mutual recognition.

At long last, both the Berlin problem and the German question had been solved. Everyone finally agreed that Germany and Berlin would remain divided.

Unification

The situation remained much this way until 1989. Then, as a result primarily of new Soviet foreign-policy attitudes, change came rapidly. In September 1989, hundreds of thousands of East Germans demanding reform took to the streets in Leipzig and East Berlin. In October, East German leader Honecker resigned, but the demonstrations only grew larger. In November, the entire East German government and then the East German Communist Party's Politburo resigned. On November 9, a reconstituted communist government lifted all travel restrictions to the West. Immediately, East Berliners and West Berliners climbed the Berlin Wall and breached it. An era had ended.

Even more change was to come. In February 1990, the East German and West German governments met in Ottawa, Canada, and agreed that East Germany should become part of West Germany. The Soviet Union accepted the concept of German unification under a West German government in July. Two months later, France, Great Britain, the United States, the Soviet Union, and the two German governments signed the "Two Plus Four" Agreement arranging the unification of Germany. East Germany adopted the West German mark on July 1, 1990. Then, on October 3, 1990, East and West Germany unified under the West German government, and forty-five years of German division came to an end. Germany was again a single united nation-state.

At first, euphoria swept Germany and Western Europe. Then the realization set in that the German question again faced the European continent. This time, it could be posed as, "What does German unification mean for Europe in the 1990s and beyond?"

Germany and the Future

The major concern in the minds of most Europeans concerning German unification was whether a newly-united Germany might revert once again to the chauvinistic and expansionist policies that had led to World Wars I and II. Almost without exception, West Germans assured their European neighbors that this could not happen.

For nearly half a century, most West Germans argued, their country had been a model democracy. A flourishing multiparty political system was in place, and the government had acted responsibly and humanely toward its citizenry and visitors. Most West Germans asserted that such actions, outlooks, and values were now ingrained, and that unification would have no adverse impact on Germany's exemplary behavior.

Nevertheless, some skeptics remained concerned that Germany might revert to old habits. Skeptics saw the wave of attacks on foreigners that swept Germany in 1992 and 1993 as proof that Germany had not reformed completely. Conversely, those who believed that a new Germany was in place pointed out that the attacks had been launched by a small fringe element in Germany, and that hundreds of thousands of Germans had protested against the attacks. They also noted that the German government had heatedly condemned the attacks, and that in the early 1990s, such attacks were not exclusively a German phenomenon. They occurred in France, Spain, and elsewhere as well.

At the same time, many other Germans and some non-German Europeans wondered whether German unification could be successfully achieved. The West German government itself was stunned at how old and out-of-date the East German industrial structure was, and at how much it would cost to make East German industry competitive again. In addition, the East German communication and transportation infrastructures were woefully inadequate for the needs of a modern industrial state. In all respects, the economic costs of unification would be much greater than originally imagined, and unification would take much longer than originally expected as well.

Equally perplexing was the loss in work ethic that had developed under the East German communist regime. Used to having a guaranteed job and a guaranteed income, some East Germans seemed to have lost the drive and ambition that was once associated simply with "being German." This was completely unexpected, and came as a shock to many West Germans. In many cases, it also led to the growth of considerable West German antipathy toward their new countrymen.

Conversely, other East Germans were willing to work long hours for low wages now that they had the opportunity to better their lives. Ironically, they too were sometimes resented, primarily because of their willingness to work hard for low wages.

Despite the economic and social problems that Germany experienced with unification, many Europeans took a more long-range view. They became concerned that once German unification had been achieved and East Germany had achieved West German standards, Germany would become an economic juggernaut that would rule Europe economically if not politically. This outlook changed some people's attitudes about the wisdom of German unification.

Others who believed that a united Germany would inevitably grow economically more powerful viewed the issue in the context of the European Community (EC). From this perspective, they reached two diametrically opposed conclusions. To some, Germany's future economic growth would lead to German political and economic domination of the EC (later the European Union, or EU). Thus, they argued, German unity had changed the calculus of the EC. EC unity should be abandoned and EC integration rethought, they asserted.

Others argued that the possibility of overwhelming future German political and economic power made it all the more necessary to tie Europe and Germany firmly together in a united European Union. Better to have a dominant Germany constrained by involvement with the EU, they argued, than to have an unconstrained Germany doing as it pleased throughout Europe.

Obviously, by 1994, various dimensions of the German question had resurfaced in Europe. German unification, once viewed in the West as a solution to many European issues, had solved some problems, but it had also raised others anew.

Issues for the U.S. and the World

The unification of East and West Germany into a single country in 1990 was a clear signal that the Cold War was over, and that a new era was about to begin. But German unification also raised a number of difficult questions for Europe, the United States, and the world. Some of the issues addressed on the SCIS Videotape "Europe After the Cold War," Lesson 4, "The German Question," by the former Secretaries and by the former world leaders include:

1. **Germany's history.** Germany has emerged as a democratic country with a strong commitment to democratic ideals and principles. Why, then, did the idea of German unification raise so many questions about the future of Germany? How did the German government try to address these questions? How concerned were the former Secretaries and world leaders about these questions? Why do you believe they feel the way that they do?

2. **Germany's economic strength.** Secretary Vance says that he sees Germany emerging as the dominant economic power in Europe. Former German Chancellor Schmidt has a considerably different perspective. How and why do the two men differ about Germany's economic role and Germany's economic strength? Whom do you believe is right? Why?

3. **a British perspective on Germany.** Former British Prime Minister James Callaghan offers an assessment of Germany from the viewpoint of the leader of another European country. What is Callaghan's perspective on Germany? What are his concerns? Do you think that his ideas reflect the thoughts of leaders of other European countries about Germany?

4. **German unification and the future.** What does German unification mean for the future of Europe, and for the future of the European Community? What does it mean for U.S. policy regarding Europe?

Selected Bibliography

Balfour, Michael. Germany: The Tides of Power (New York: Routledge, 1992).

Dalton, Russell J. Politics in Germany (New York: Harper Collins, 1992).

Fulbrook, Mary. The Divided Nation: A History of Germany, 1918-1990 (New York: Oxford University Press, 1992).

James, Harold, and Marla Stone. (Editors), When the Wall Came Down: Reactions to German Unification (New York: Routledge, 1992).

Kirchner, Emil J., and James Sperling. The Federal Republic of Germany and NATO (New York: St. Martins, 1991).

Paterson, William E., and David Southern. Governing Germany (Cambridge, MA: Harvard University Press, 1991).

Paterson, William E., and David Spence. (Editors), German Unification (Cambridge, MA: Blackwell, 1993).

Smyser, W.R. Germany and America: New Identities, Fateful Rift? (Boulder, CO: Westview, 1993).

Treverton, Gregory F. America, Germany, and the Future of Europe (Princeton, NJ: Princeton University Press, 1993).

Verheyen, Dirk, and Christian Soe. (Editors), The Germans and Their Neighbors (Boulder, CO: Westview, 1993).

LESSON 4

THE GERMAN QUESTION

Activity 1:

HOW DO GOVERNMENTAL LEADERS SEE "THE GERMAN QUESTION"?

ACTIVITY OBJECTIVE

The student will be aware of and understand the sources of several of the different perspectives that exist about German unification.

MATERIALS AND RESOURCES

❑   Worksheet 4.1 "Government Leaders and the German Question"

❑   SCIS Videotape "Europe After the Cold War," Lesson 4, "The German Question"

STRATEGIES

Because of former historical events such as the Franco-Prussian War, World War I, and World War II, many people are concerned that Germany has become such a powerful country. This lesson gives students the opportunity to review several different opinions concerning the future role of the united Germany, which is referred to as "The German Question." Distribute Worksheet 4.1 "Government Leaders and the German Question," and point out the different time periods in which each served in government. Write the following two quotations on the board and have students identify the author and possible meaning when they come up in the video:

- "I'm very glad that Germany's not going to be a neutral state rolling like a loose cannon around the decks of Europe."

  Dean Rusk expressing concern about the new power being wielded by a unified Germany.

- "...Germany could then carry us down roads that the rest of us would not wish to go."

  James Callaghan expressing concern about the economic control Germany could exert over the other EC member states.

While the SCIS Videotape "Europe After the Cold War," Lesson 4, "The German Question," is being played, ask students to complete Worksheet 4.1 including phrases and/or statements supporting their answers about the leaders' perspectives.

Afterwards, discuss the position of each leader on unification and European integration, calling on students to support their answers. Then, pose the following questions for discussion:

- At the beginning of the video excerpt of the 1989 Secretaries of State conference, Hedrick Smith summarizes the concern of Secretaries Rusk and Haig that other countries of Europe might not support a unified Germany. In light of recent events taking place in Europe and discussions later on the tape, were such concerns warranted? Why or why not?

  Answers may vary. Some Europeans still fear the power of a united Germany even though the German government has maintained peaceful and cooperative relationships with other states.

- In the mid-twentieth century, Germany was feared for its military power. For what reasons might Germany be feared in the twenty-first century? What evidence does Helmut Schmidt provide to dispel such fear?

  Germany is even now feared for its economic power. Schmidt attempts to reassure the audience by citing the massive rebuilding campaign that must bring the former East Germany on par with the West before Germany is able to develop into a financial superpower. He also reminds Callaghan that as a member of the European Community, Germany is contributing to the development of Europe as a whole and should not be thought of as competing with other EC members.

After having students compare perspectives of various leaders on German unification, discuss with the class whether Germany should be feared more today than just prior to unification in 1990 or should it be feared less. Activity 2 will provide more information about the historical background and consequences of German unification.

GOVERNMENT LEADERS
AND THE GERMAN QUESTION

NAME OF POLITICAL LEADER	POSITION ON GERMAN UNIFICATION	POSITION ON EUROPEAN INTEGRATION
Alexander Haig		
Cyrus Vance		
Dean Rusk		
Helmut Schmidt		
James Callaghan		

LESSON 4

THE GERMAN QUESTION

Activity 2:

WHAT EFFECTS HAS GERMAN UNIFICATION HAD ON GERMANY AND ON EUROPE?

ACTIVITY OBJECTIVE

The student will develop an understanding of the impact that German unification has had on Germany and on Europe.

MATERIALS AND RESOURCES

❑ SCIS Videotape "Europe After the Cold War," Lesson 4, "The German Question"

❑ Worksheet 4.2 "Historical Analysis of German Unification"

❑ Handout 4.1 "Changing German Borders"

❑ Handout 4.2 "Unification of Germany: Cold War Reflections"

❑ Handout 4.3 "Currency Crisis Hits European Community"

❑ Worksheet 4.3 "State Department Memorandum"

❑ Handout 4.4 "Unification of Germany: The Future"

STRATEGIES

Before beginning this lesson, assemble copies of the following resource sheets into the number of groups of five students you have in your classroom:

- Worksheet 4.2 "Historical Analysis of German Unification"
- Handout 4.1 "Changing German Borders (pages 1-6)"
- Handout 4.2 "Unification of Germany: Cold War Reflections"
- Handout 4.3 "Currency Crisis Hits EC"
- Worksheet 4.3 "State Department Memo"
- Handout 4.5 "Unification of Germany: The Future"

Assign students to groups of five and distribute to each group a folder containing the above items. Show students Lesson 4 of the SCIS videotape to set the tone for the rest of the activity. Then, have each group follow instructions on Worksheet 4.2 "Historical Analysis of German Unification." Individual and peer assessment can be used to evaluate performance of group roles and contribution to final group product/presentation.

HISTORICAL ANALYSIS OF GERMAN UNIFICATION

Directions for small groups

I. Distribute pages 1-6 of Handout 4.1 "Changing German Borders" to different group members and compare the borders of Germany at different time periods. Write a group paragraph that describes the changing borders of Germany.

II. Watch the SCIS Videotape "Europe After the Cold War," Part 4, "The German Question," as a group. Pay attention to the use of the word "reunification." Alexander Haig and others in the video use the term "reunification" to describe what transpired in Germany in 1990. On the back of this page write an explanation of how the use of the term "reunification" by the Secretaries is geographically inaccurate.

One group member should appoint members to take turns reading aloud Handout 4.2 "Unification of Germany: Cold War Reflections." Explain how the term "reunification" can be viewed as accurate in a political sense. Brainstorm how a nation's currency reflects its identity and unity. Based on Handout 4.2, "Unification of Germany: Cold War Reflections," describe how actions concerning German currency have affected its post-war occupation. Write your answer.

III. As a group read Handout 4.3 "Currency Crisis Hits EC." What does this news summary indicate about the role of the German mark and economy relative to that of other Western European countries? Pretend that you represent a team of analysts at the U.S. Department of State. Use Worksheet 4.3 "State Department Memorandum" to write a one-page brief outlining the impact of this event on U.S. economic and political interests in Europe.

IV. As a group read Handout 4.4 "Unification of Germany: The Future." Pretend that the group represents political advisers to Chancellor Helmut Kohl of Germany. Research and discuss each of the following political challenges, collecting current events and information about each one:

   A. Alienation of other European neighbors over the 1993 currency crisis.

   B. Growing hostility between former East and West German residents.

   C. Worldwide fear of the growing economic power of a united Germany.

As a group compose a two-paragraph recommendation on each of the above challenges. Send a group "checker" to other groups to share information and to hear their recommendations as well. Prepare a two-minute oral presentation with visual aid to reinforce the group's recommendation. The teacher will play the role of the Chancellor of Germany and will call on groups to give presentations on one of the three political challenges. Assessment will be based on realistic analysis of current resources and conditions existing in Germany and Europe, clarity and originality of presentation, and group cooperation and involvement in the final product.

CHANGING GERMAN BORDERS

The German States in 1810

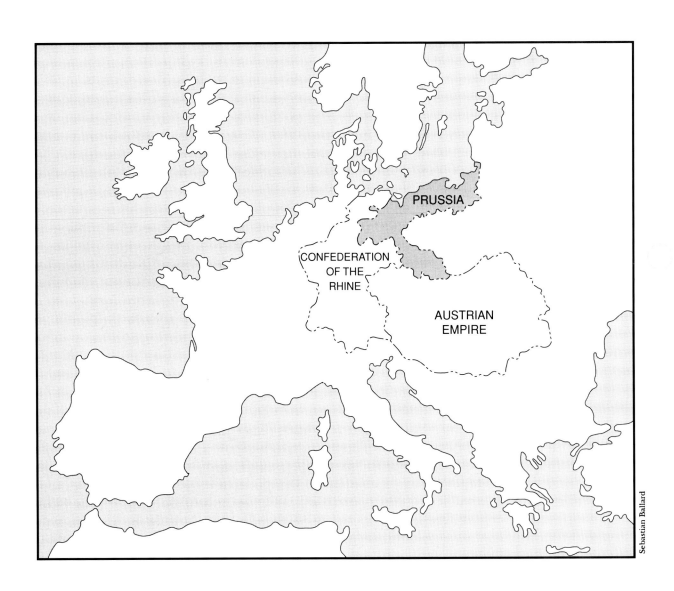

CHANGING GERMAN BORDERS

The German States in 1815

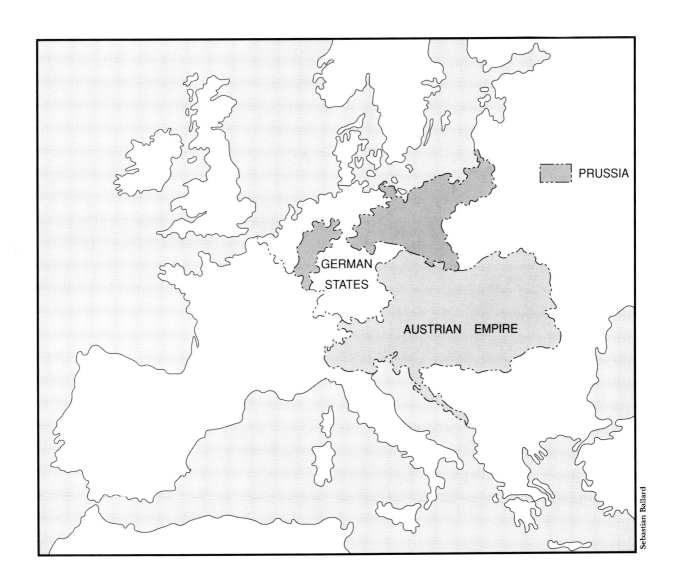

Sebastian Ballard

119

CHANGING GERMAN BORDERS

The German Empire 1871-1918

CHANGING GERMAN BORDERS

Germany 1919-1937

CHANGING GERMAN BORDERS

Germany Divided 1945-1990

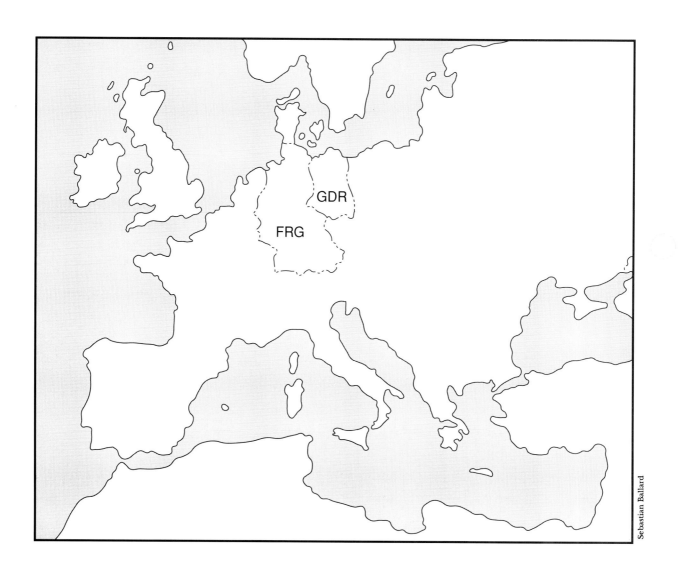

122

CHANGING GERMAN BORDERS

United Germany in Europe   1990 - Today

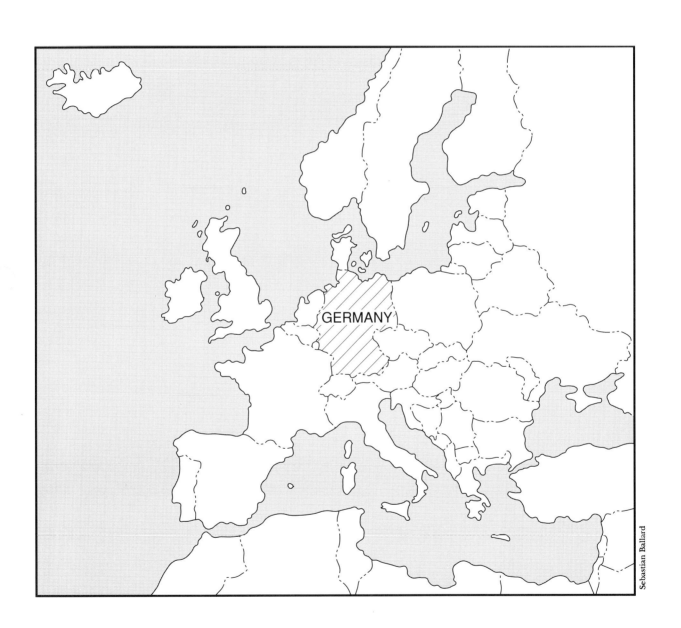

123

UNIFICATION OF GERMANY: COLD WAR REFLECTIONS

To understand how Germany was unified, one must begin with its division after World War II. At the Yalta Conference just before the end of the war, the United States, the Soviet Union, and the United Kingdom agreed that they as well as France should split Germany into four zones of occupation. Each occupying country would be responsible for administering all affairs within its zone. Berlin, Germany's capital situated deep within the Soviet occupation zone, would also be divided into four parts. It was agreed that all four zones of both Berlin and the rest of Germany would eventually be unified. Until then, all major decisions affecting Germany were to be made by the four-power "Allied Control Commission" in Berlin.

There were two major issues relating to Germany that soon drove the Soviet Union and its former allies apart. The first was Germany's future political orientation and the second was the economic question of reparations. While the intention of the Western Allies was to create a democratic Germany, the Soviets worked to establish a pro-Soviet communist government in their eastern zone.

At the Potsdam Conference in July 1945, the new U.S. president, Harry Truman, proposed that the $20 billion of reparations which had been discussed at Yalta serve only as a figure for further discussion. He also suggested that reparations be taken by each country from its respective zone of occupation, not from Germany as a whole. The Soviets objected to both points, and deadlock resulted. In the end, because no peace conference was held to end World War II, Germany remained under occupation with the three western allies working to unite their zones and the U.S.S.R. consolidating control over its zone.

The final break came when the Western powers instituted a currency reform to accelerate economic recovery in the three zones. The Soviets viewed this as a threat, and blockaded all land access routes to communist-surrounded West Berlin. For the eleven months that followed, U.S., British, and French pilots flew in all of the needs of West Berlin. Although the Soviets eventually reopened land transportation routes to the capital, Germany remained divided for the next forty-five years. Throughout that period, the two parts of Germany developed different political, economic, and social systems.

In East Germany (the German Democratic Republic), an autocratic political system and a centralized economic system developed. In West Germany (the Federal Republic of Germany), a multi-party democratic political system and a free-market economy emerged. Between 1945 and 1969, official West German and Western policy remained unyielding to seek total unification of Germany. However, the reality of the situation was that no government expected unification, and none wanted it except as defined by its own terms.

Then, between 1970 and 1972, treaties were signed in which East and West Germany renounced unification and mutually recognized each other's boundaries. Peaceful coexistence remained in place between East and West until 1989 when cracks in the East German Communist Party and changed Soviet government policies allowed protests against the Honecker government of East Germany to go unchecked. In September 1989, hundreds of thousands of East Germans demanding reform took to the streets in Leipzig and East Berlin. In October, Honecker resigned. Nevertheless, the protests grew larger. In November, the entire East German government and Communist Party Politburo resigned. On November 9, 1989, all travel restrictions to the West were lifted. Immediately, East and West Berliners assaulted and breached the Berlin Wall.

From that day forward, changes came so fast to Germany that many world leaders were caught off guard by them. In February 1990, the East German and West German governments met in Ottawa and agreed that East Germany should become part of West Germany. The Soviet Union accepted the concept of German unification under a West German government in July. Two months later, France, the United Kingdom, the United States, the Soviet Union, and the two German governments signed the "Two Plus Four" Agreement arranging the unification of Germany. Then, on October 3, 1990, forty-five years of German division came to an end. Germany was once again a single united nation-state.

CURRENCY CRISIS HITS EUROPEAN COMMUNITY: NEWS SUMMARY

Tuesday, August 3, 1993. After the French franc dropped over 2% in world currency trading, European governments were left wondering what was left of their monetary system and the EC's plan to create a single currency by 1999. Danish, Belgian, Spanish and Portuguese money all lost value against the German mark and Dutch guilder. This event marked the most serious setback to the European Monetary System since its creation in 1979.

Between early 1992 and mid-1993, the complicated formula of currency integration had been viewed as critical to the eventual adoption of a single currency. However, this system collapsed in late July and early August 1993 after the German central bank refused to lower its key interest rates. Much to the dismay of the French government, speculators quickly began dumping the weaker currencies in favor of the stronger mark. In response to French criticism, German Bundesbank officials said that they were concerned about growing inflation in their own country due to the massive economic assistance program taking place in the former East Germany.

Rather than authorize a full free market in the trading of their currencies, EC finance ministers widened the margins to 15% above or below nominal exchange values so that the seven currencies could fluctuate. The ministers insisted that such a move was temporary and that they remained committed to the creation of a single currency as early as 1997 and no later than 1999. This is one of the major objectives of the Maastricht Treaty on European union. The United Kingdom became the last EC member to ratify the treaty on Monday, August 2.

Ironically, the crash of the European monetary system may mean that Europe's depressed economies will recover sooner rather than later. As conditions worsened during the past three years, the European Community countries' hopes of recovery became tangled in the so-called Exchange Rate Mechanism, a procedure designed to limit currency fluctuations. The ERM's purpose was to tie the various currencies closely to one another, ending the panicky devaluation and financial chaos of the past. It was supposed to serve as an interim step to a single European currency by the end of the decade.

But in practice, monetary coordination allowed EC's strongest member, Germany, to dictate currency policy for most of Europe. Due to the reluctance of German Bundesbank officials to lower interest rates, it was difficult for struggling businesses in the rest of Europe to borrow much-needed capital to stay afloat during the lingering recession. Most politicians and industrialists desired an anti-recession strategy that included a big slash in interest rates that has been taking place in the United States. But as long as their currencies were tied to the German mark by ERM rules, European governments had little choice but to follow Bundesbank policy.

Sensing that the ERM would fall apart sooner or later, rich speculators began trading other currencies for German marks. This lower demand made such currencies worth less overall, and the EC finance ministers hurriedly scheduled a meeting in Brussels to work out a solution. Meantime, the devalued currencies have made products of France and other nations better buys for Americans and other consumers. Economic experts feel that once the current recession lifts in Europe, EC members will again return to the schedule for currency integration. For the moment, however, the process is on hold.

Adapted from: Kaplan, Bernard D., "Monetary shake-up to hasten recovery of EC's economies," <u>Atlanta Journal</u>, August 3, 1993, page E3.

STATE DEPARTMENT MEMORANDUM

INTEROFFICE MEMORANDUM

TO: **Deputy Secretary for European Affairs**
U.S. Department of State

FROM: _____ **Desk**

SUBJECT: **Concerns Related to European Currency Crisis**

UNIFICATION OF GERMANY: THE FUTURE

The initial euphoria surrounding the fall of the Berlin Wall and unification was short-lived for most Germans. They had been promised a relatively painless process of bringing East Germany into the "fold" of the Federal Republic of Germany. What they found was an East German industrial system that was out-of-date, and communication and transportation infrastructures that could not be integrated with a modern industrial structure. In addition, many who had fled the communist East when Germany was divided began to return to the former East Germany to claim property and housing that the former East German government had long ago redistributed.

While these challenges were daunting, an even more perplexing phenomenon soon developed. Used to having guaranteed jobs and incomes under communist rule, some East Germans no longer had the same drive and ambition as their fellow citizens in the West. Part of this was the result of the economic uncertainty and chaos that pervaded the former East as a result of unification. Conversely, some East Germans were willing to work long hours for low wages now that they had an opportunity to better their own lives. In both cases, this led to some hostility toward these newly reinstated citizens of the Federal Republic of Germany. At the same time, in West Germany, taxes began to rise. Thus, the process of unification began to grow painful.

Outside Germany, many Europeans began to look with concern at the "new" Germany. They became concerned that once German unification was achieved and East Germany had achieved West German standards, Germany would become an economic juggernaut that would dominate Europe economically if not politically. This outlook changed some people's attitudes about the wisdom of German unification. Some argued that such growth would lead to German control of the European Community (EC). This led some to reassess their support of the EC. Others asserted that such growth was all the more reason to tie Germany to an integrated Europe. An unconstrained Germany doing as it pleased, they said, was potentially a greater menace.

Then, there were the attacks on foreigners that swept Germany in 1992 and 1993. Although such attacks also took place in several other countries in Western Europe, many people feared that the attacks that took place in Germany suggested that at least part of German society was returning to the racism of the Nazi past. However, those who believed that a new Germany was in place were quick to point out that such attacks had been launched by a small fringe element in Germany, and that hundreds of thousands of Germans had taken to the streets to protest such violence. They also pointed out that the German government had heatedly condemned each and every attack, and that in the early 1990s such attacks were not exclusively a German phenomenon.

In the end, the adage, "Be careful what you ask for, you might get it," seems to apply to the European perspective on German unification. Once viewed in the West as a solution to many European issues, German unification now has raised new questions and concerns. Once again Germany has become a major player on the world stage.

LESSON 5

EUROPEAN SECURITY

Lesson 5 of 6 Lesson Plans for the
Southern Center for International Studies'
High School Educational Package
EUROPE AFTER THE COLD WAR

NATO has long been the central focus of Western European security. But with the end of the Cold War, what security issues confront Europe and how can they best be met? Here, Italian and Portuguese troops participate in NATO maneuvers in northern Italy.

Study Guide for

**LESSON 5
of the SCIS Educational Package
*EUROPE AFTER THE COLD WAR***

EUROPEAN SECURITY

Since shortly after the end of World War II, the paramount security concern of every country in Western Europe was whether or not the Soviet Union and its allies would militarily invade Western Europe. Because of this concern, European and North Atlantic security organizations such as the North Atlantic Treaty Organization (NATO) and the Western European Union (WEU) were established; large numbers of American troops and large quantities of U.S. military equipment were deployed in Europe; and the United States took the leadership position in planning for and arranging the security of Europe.

However, as Mikhail Gorbachev began to institute his revolution in the Soviet Union after 1985, the Soviet threat to Western European security began to recede. The Eastern European revolutions of 1989 reduced the long-time Soviet threat still more. By 1990, the Soviet threat had dissipated so much that NATO restated its defense doctrine, declaring that it no longer considered the Soviet Union an enemy. Some people disagreed with this formula, but the following year, the Soviet Union broke up. The Soviet threat was gone.

But did the end of the Soviet Union mean that there were no more threats to European security? If it did, did this then imply that alliances like NATO and the WEU that had been set up to counter the Soviet threat should be dismantled? Or were there other threats that these alliances could be reconfigured to cope with? If so, what were they? Or, rather, if there were other threats to European security, were new security organizations needed? Indeed, in the post–Cold War world, what did European security mean?

European Security in the 1990s

The most basic element of security is the ability to deter a direct military attack against oneself, and in the event of a failure of deterrence, to repulse the attack. With the demise of the Soviet Union, the only sizeable realistic military threat directed against Europe disappeared. Thus, in the world of the mid-1990s, Europe appears completely secure from any sizeable external military attack.

This does not mean that Europe's present or future security is guaranteed. On the immediate scene, terrorism remains a threat. So too does the possibility of ethnic or political violence within individual European states. Especially dangerous is the possibility of such violence spilling over from one state to another. Europe also has economic-related security concerns, most notably its dependency on external energy resources. Only Great Britain and Norway are self-sufficient in oil.

On a more abstract level, security also deals with implementing current policies and constructing present institutions so that the possibility of future threats to security are minimized. Thus, even as European leaders plan to meet present security challenges in the absence of a sizeable realistic military threat, they must also fashion policies and institutions that reduce the possibility of future threats materializing.

In the post–Cold War world, how should this be done? One useful place to begin to answer this question is to examine security and security-related organizations that Europe already has in place.

NATO, the WEU and the CSCE

Currently, there are three major security and security-related organizations in place in Europe. The most important in terms of military capabilities is the 16-member North Atlantic Treaty Organization (NATO), which served as the primary Western European bulwark against a feared Soviet attack on Western Europe from its inception in 1949 until the U.S.S.R.'s collapse in 1991. Belgium, Canada, Denmark, France, Germany, Great Britain, Greece, Iceland, Italy, Luxembourg, the Netherlands, Norway, Portugal, Spain, Turkey, and the United States are the members of NATO.

The Western European Union (WEU) is the oldest security organization in Europe. Founded in 1948 under the Brussels Treaty by Belgium, France, Luxembourg, Great Britain, and the Netherlands, with West Germany and Italy joining in 1954, the WEU was dormant for most of the Cold War, superceded by NATO. However, the WEU began to revive in the late 1980s when NATO's European members became increasingly concerned about the need to create a "European leg" for NATO. In December 1991, the Maastricht Treaty declared that the WEU might become either the "European pillar" of NATO or the defense arm of the European Community.

The third security-related organization in Europe is the Conference of Security and Cooperation in Europe (CSCE). Begun in 1973 by 35 European and North American states, the CSCE had expanded by 1993 to include 51 states. The expansion was the result of the break-up of the Soviet Union, Yugoslavia, and Czechoslovakia, all of whose constituent elements as independent states joined the CSCE.

Until 1991, the CSCE required unanimous consent before it could even discuss an issue. However, even if it discussed an issue, the CSCE had no means to act. In addition to discussing European security issues and seeking to promote ways to cooperate, the CSCE also included human rights as one of its primary issues of concern.

All three of these organizations were created during the Cold War to approach specific Cold War problems. Therefore, with the Cold War over, it may reasonably be asked if all three have not outlived their usefulness.

To examine this question, we must first ask whether NATO, the WEU, or the CSCE did more during the Cold War than approach East-West problems. If they did, we must ask whether these other tasks remain relevant in the post–Cold War world. Given that all three institutions are in place and operating today, we must also ask whether they need be or can be modified to respond to Europe's current and future security challenges.

In NATO's case, the organization in fact did more than deter the U.S.S.R. and the Warsaw Pact. Throughout the Cold War, NATO also served as a forum that coordinated and integrated the defense policies of Western European and North American states. NATO therefore was much more than an anti-Soviet alliance.

At the same time, NATO served as an effective way to control West Germany's military. With its military planning and force build-up taking place firmly within the context of NATO, West Germany contributed to its own defense without raising concerns among its neighbors about the rebirth of German militarism. Given the history of the German question, this was one of NATO's major accomplishments.

Since the collapse of the Soviet Union, NATO has also taken on an additional task, creating what amounts to a "half-way house" to discuss the security concerns of Eastern European states and Soviet successor states. This half-way house, called the North Atlantic Coordination Council (NACC), is designed as a forum at which the security concerns of all NATO, former Warsaw Pact, and Soviet successor states can be discussed without extending the security guarantees of NATO to any non-NATO member. NACC may best be seen as an organization associated with NATO whose purpose is to build confidence between all of its member states.

Despite NACC, several Eastern European states expressed desires to become full members of NATO. The United States and several other NATO states resisted this, not wanting to raise Russian concerns that NATO might still present a threat to Russian security. Thus, during President Bill Clinton's January 1994 trip to Europe, he proposed a new "Partnership for Peace" program that would bring Eastern European states into closer cooperation with NATO, but not make them full members nor extend NATO's security guarantees to them.

Despite these additional accomplishments, serious questions remain about NATO. Its primary purpose was undeniably to deter the Soviet Union. It fulfilled this task admirably. With the passing of the U.S.S.R., regardless of what else it has achieved, many people still question whether NATO should continue to exist.

The Western European Union finds itself in a somewhat different position. For most of its existence, the WEU has done little or nothing. Long overshadowed by NATO, many Europeans now see the WEU as the European component of NATO, or as the defense arm of the European Community. In either regard, they consider a revitalized WEU as an appropriate response to changing international conditions.

However, there are many people on both sides of the Atlantic that are uncomfortable with this. First, many Europeans and Americans alike are concerned that the establishment of an effective WEU might undermine NATO, and in so doing, undermine European-American cooperation. This would be a tragedy of the highest order, they argue. Others point out that the WEU has never been effective, and that all EC members and all European NATO members are not included within the WEU. At best, they assert, the WEU could therefore provide only partial and untested defense.

As for the CSCE, it too is undergoing significant changes. In 1990, the CSCE began to create for itself a limited framework of institutions that might allow it to deal with international crises. These institutions included a Council of Foreign Ministers of all member states that was to meet annually, a permanent secretariat, and a conflict-prevention center. But by 1993, the CSCE still had not dealt meaningfully with a single

European crisis, and whether or not it would ever be able to deal effectively with security issues remained an open question.

However, in all fairness, given the past performance of other European security and security-related institutions in the post–Cold War world, the CSCE was not the only institution that had a less than exemplary track record.

European Security and the United States

The end of the Cold War and the rapid changes of the late 1980s and the early 1990s in Europe raised questions not only about the viability and relevance of European security institutions, but also about the American role in Europe. In the late 1940s, in the presence of a perceived Soviet threat to Western Europe, the United States for the first time in its history entered a military alliance during peacetime, the North Atlantic Treaty. In the early 1950s, in the face of a perceived growth in the Soviet threat to Western Europe, it deployed troops and equipment to Western Europe. The American commitment to Europe was real and undebatable.

But by 1992, the Soviet threat was gone, and Europe was changing. Why should the U.S. keep its troops and equipment in Europe? Even more pointedly, did the United States any longer have any interests in Europe?

Some people termed "neo-isolationists," argued that the U.S. no longer had major interests in Europe, and the time had come to withdraw U.S. troops from Europe. To them, the time had come to concentrate on American domestic problems. Others who opposed the U.S. presence in Europe, or who wished to see the level of U.S. commitment there reduced, were not neo-isolationists, but they wanted the U.S. to concentrate elsewhere. They argued that the center of global economic growth was now the Pacific, and that that was where the United States should concentrate.

Still others reached different conclusions. The U.S. retained extensive interests in Europe, not the least of which was continued European stability, they said. Twice before in the twentieth century, the United States had been drawn into European wars. Given that most Europeans saw the United States as a source of stability in Europe, advocates of continued U.S. military presence in Europe asked why the U.S. should withdraw from Europe. Did not the historical record argue that Europe needed stability?

In addition, advocates of continued U.S. presence in Europe observed that the U.S. had significant economic and cultural ties with Europe that could not be abandoned. Nor should it be overlooked, they pointed out, that U.S. troops and equipment in Europe offered a convenient "jumping-off point" for deployment elsewhere, most noticeably in the Middle East. Indeed, many of the U.S. forces that participated in Operations Desert Shield and Desert Storm in 1990 and 1991 against Iraq were based in Europe.

So the debate rages on. Does the United States still have security interests in Europe, or have changing European conditions and the end of the Cold War significantly reduced or even eliminated U.S. security interests there? This is only one of many unanswered questions about Europe's future.

Issues for the U.S. and the World

The end of the Cold War, German unification, and the break-up of the Soviet Union clearly mean that global security concerns are shifting. No longer is Europe and the world divided into East and West, and no longer does any single security threat loom over Europe and the United States.

But this does not mean that threats to European and U.S. security no longer exist. In the SCIS Videotape "Europe After the Cold War," Lesson 5, "European Security," the former Secretaries address several important issues relating to European security and their implications for the United States. These issues include:

1. **the role and future of NATO.** Former Secretaries Rusk and Muskie both believe that NATO has been successful as an alliance. Former Secretary Kissinger also believes it has been successful, but argues that it should redefine its objectives. Why do the former Secretaries assert that NATO has been a success? Why does Secretary Muskie believe that it will be difficult to sustain NATO? What new goals and missions does Secretary Kissinger recommend for the alliance?

2. **the future of the security relationship between the United States and Europe.** What do Secretaries Vance and Kissinger believe should be the security relationship between the U.S. and Europe? Why does Secretary Rogers disagree, and what is his position on the issue? With whom do you agree? Why?

3. **nuclear weapons in Europe.** Secretary Haig observed that nuclear weapons were a particular problem in Europe. Why did he see this as a problem? How did German unification affect this issue? What is the current status of nuclear weapons in Europe?

4. **the structure of future European security organizations.** With the end of the East-West conflict, some people believe that the Western European Union or the Conference on Security and Cooperation in Europe should replace NATO as the primary security structure in and for the states of Europe. How do you believe the former Secretaries would respond to these suggestions? Why? What are the strengths and weaknesses of the WEU and the CSCE as security organizations? What would the implications of the replacement of NATO by either the WEU or the CSCE as the primary European security structure be for the United States?

Selected Bibliography

Brady, Linda P. The Politics of Negotiation: America's Dealings with Allies, Adversaries, and Friends (Chapel Hill, NC: University of North Carolina Press, 1991).

Brauch, Hans Gunter, and Robert Kennedy. (Editors), Alternative Conventional Defense Postures in the European Theater Volume 2: The Impact of Political Change on Strategy, Technology, and Arms Control (Washington, DC: Crane Russack, 1992).

Brauch, Hans Gunter, and Robert Kennedy. (Editors), Alternative Conventional Defense Postures in the European Theater Volume 3: Force Posture Alternatives for Europe After the Cold War (Washington, D.: Crane Russack, 1993).

Feld, Werner J. The Future of European Security and Defense Policy (Boulder, CO: Lynne Rienner Publishers, 1993).

Freedman, Lawrence. (Editor), Europe Transformed: Documents on the End of the Cold War (New York: St. Martins, 1990).

Haftendorn, Helga, and Christian Tuschhoff. (Editors), America and Europe in an Era of Change (Boulder, CO: Westview, 1993).

Hogan, Michael J. (Editor), The End of the Cold War: Its Meaning and Implications (New York: Cambridge University Press, 1992).

Kelleher, Catherine M. Germany and the Politics of Nuclear Weapons (New York: Columbia University Press, 1975).

North Atlantic Treaty Organization. The North Atlantic Treaty Organization: Facts and Figures (Brussels: NATO Information Service, 1991).

Simon, Jeffrey. (Editor), European Security Policy After the Revolutions of 1989 (Washington, DC: National Defense University, 1991).

Wharton, William D. (Editor), European Security Arrangements for the 1990s and Beyond (Washington, DC: National Defense University, 1992).

LESSON 5

EUROPEAN SECURITY

Activity 1:

WHAT IS THE ROLE OF NATO, THE WEU AND THE CSCE?

ACTIVITY OBJECTIVE

The student will be able to identify, describe, and explain the purposes of the three security-related organizations in Europe.

MATERIALS AND RESOURCES

❏ Handout 5.1 "Security-Related Organizations in Europe"

❏ Handout 5.2 "Membership of Various Organizations"

❏ Worksheet 5.1 "Data Retrieval Chart"

❏ Worksheet 5.2 "Format for Critiquing Articles on European Security Organizations"

❏ Current newspapers, news magazines, news analysis materials, Reader's Guide to Periodical Literature

STRATEGIES

Make arrangements for students to go to the media center to conduct research. Have each student locate an article on one of the following security organizations: North Atlantic Treaty Organization (NATO), Western European Union (WEU), and Conference of Security and Cooperation in Europe (CSCE). You may need to have students work in small groups if resources are scarce. Once they have located an article, provide Worksheet 5.2, "Format for Critiquing Articles" to help guide the students as they read the article.

Distribute to students Handouts 5.1 "Security-Related Organizations in Europe" and 5.2 "Membership of Various Organizations" which contain information on the three security-related organizations in Europe. Have students read and study the handouts. Distribute Worksheet 5.1, "Data Retrieval Chart."

Using the information from the two handouts, have students complete the chart. Then discuss the answers to the questions at the end of Handout 5.1. Provide time for students to share their articles with the class. A similar format can be used to help students critique articles on other current topics.

SECURITY–RELATED ORGANIZATIONS IN EUROPE

At the end of World War II, the United States and Western Europe felt that there was a great need to protect Europe from any future aggression. This need to protect one-self from attack is the basic element of security. In addition, security also deals with implementing current policies and constructing present institutions so that the possibility of future threats are minimized.

Currently there are three major security-related organizations in Europe. The most important in terms of military capabilities is the 16-member North Atlantic Treaty Organization (NATO), which has served as the primary Western European protec-tion against the fear of an attack from the USSR. Belgium, Canada, Denmark, France, Germany, Great Britain, Greece, Iceland, Italy, Luxembourg, the Nether-lands, Norway, Portugal, Spain, Turkey, and the United States are members of NATO. In addition to serving as a deterrent to the USSR throughout the Cold War era, NATO also served as a forum that coordinated and integrated the defense policies of Western European and North American states. For instance, much of Europe was very afraid of Germany becoming a dominant power again. NATO served as an effective way to integrate West Germany's military within a context that was accept-able to the rest of Europe.

The Western European Union (WEU) is the oldest security organization in Europe. Founded in 1948 under the Brussels Treaty, it included Belgium, France, Luxembourg, Great Britain, and the Netherlands. West Germany and Italy joined in 1954. The WEU was inactive during most of the Cold War. However, it began to revive in the late 1980s when NATO's European members became increasingly con-cerned about the need to create a "European leg" for NATO. In December 1991, the Maastricht Treaty declared that the WEU might become either the "European pillar" of NATO or the defense arm of the European Community. There are people on both sides of the Atlantic who are uncomfortable with this. Many fear that a strong WEU might undermine European-American cooperation.

By 1990 the functions of these three organizations were being questioned. Mikhail Gorbachev had instituted his revolution in the Soviet Union, and the Soviet threat to Western European security had diminished. The Eastern European revolutions of 1989 also reduced the long-time communist threat. By 1990 the Soviet threat had dis-sipated so much that NATO restated its defense doctrine, declaring that it no longer considered the Soviet Union an enemy. In order to determine the future of these organizations there are several questions that need to be answered:

- What roles, both stated and unstated, have NATO, the WEU and the CSCE played in Europe?

- Did the end of the Soviet Union mean there are no more threats to European Security?

- Should NATO, the WEU or the CSCE be dismantled or restructured?

- Should new security organizations be created?

- In January 1994, President Clinton convinced Eastern European leaders to accept membership in a "Partnership for Peace" program that included greater cooperation with NATO, but neither full NATO membership nor security guarantees. Why did Clinton propose this? Was it good for Eastern European states? For NATO? For the U.S.? Why?

MEMBERSHIP OF VARIOUS ORGANIZATIONS

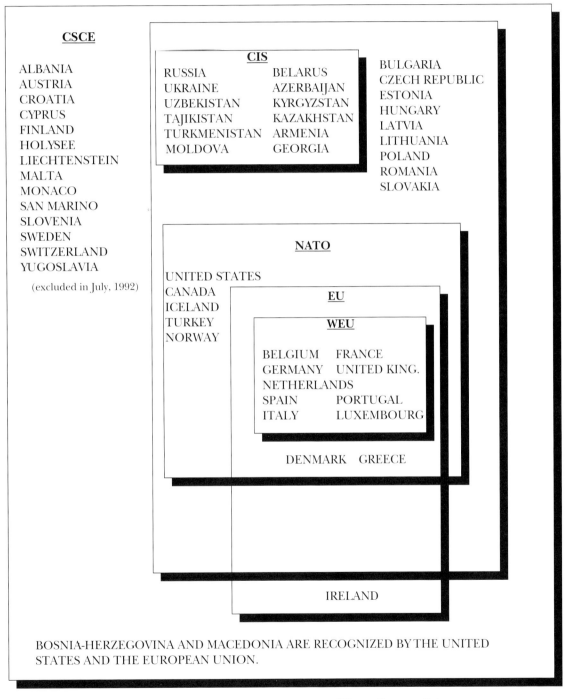

CSCE

ALBANIA
AUSTRIA
CROATIA
CYPRUS
FINLAND
HOLYSEE
LIECHTENSTEIN
MALTA
MONACO
SAN MARINO
SLOVENIA
SWEDEN
SWITZERLAND
YUGOSLAVIA

(excluded in July, 1992)

CIS

RUSSIA   BELARUS
UKRAINE   AZERBAIJAN
UZBEKISTAN   KYRGYZSTAN
TAJIKISTAN   KAZAKHSTAN
TURKMENISTAN   ARMENIA
MOLDOVA   GEORGIA

BULGARIA
CZECH REPUBLIC
ESTONIA
HUNGARY
LATVIA
LITHUANIA
POLAND
ROMANIA
SLOVAKIA

NATO

UNITED STATES
CANADA
ICELAND
TURKEY
NORWAY

EU

WEU

BELGIUM   FRANCE
GERMANY   UNITED KING.
NETHERLANDS
SPAIN   PORTUGAL
ITALY   LUXEMBOURG

DENMARK   GREECE

IRELAND

BOSNIA-HERZEGOVINA AND MACEDONIA ARE RECOGNIZED BY THE UNITED
STATES AND THE EUROPEAN UNION.

CSCE — Conference of Security and Cooperation in Europe
CIS — Commonwealth of Independent States
NATO — North Atlantic Treaty Organization

EU — European Union
WEU — Western European Union
NACC — North Atlantic Cooperation Council

DATA RETRIEVAL CHART

| MEMBERS | PURPOSE CREATED | OTHER |

	MEMBERS	PURPOSE CREATED	OTHER
NATO			
WEU			
CSCE			

FORMAT FOR CRITIQUING ARTICLES ON EUROPEAN SECURITY ORGANIZATIONS

1. What is the title of the article? Author? Date?

2. Write the title of the magazine, newspaper, government document, or book which includes the article.

3. Explain how you found the article.

4. List and briefly define any words in the article that you did not know.

5. Write a short paragraph summarizing the article.

6. List five facts that support the main ideas in the article.

7. What bias or slant did the author take on the subject of the article? Give facts to support your answer.

8. How do you feel about the purpose of this security organization?

LESSON 5

EUROPEAN SECURITY

Activity 2:

HOW WILL NATO CHANGE TO MEET PRESENT CHALLENGES IN EUROPE?

ACTIVITY OBJECTIVE

The student will be able to understand the pressures that are leading to changes in NATO, and what some of those changes may be.

MATERIALS AND RESOURCES

❑ SCIS Videotape "Europe After the Cold War," Lesson 5, "European Security"

❑ Quote from former U.S. Secretary of Defense Donald Rumsfeld

❑ Resource materials on current problems in Europe

STRATEGIES

After reading the biography of former Secretary of Defense Donald Rumsfeld to your class that can be found at the front of "Europe After the Cold War," read them the following quote from Mr. Rumsfeld:

> I've met with a group of Russian military, first when they were Soviet Union military and then later when they were Russian military. One of their comments was, "We want to be part of NATO." And of course the immediate reaction you have to this is, "Well, that's a funny thing to be saying."

Ask students why Mr. Rumsfeld might say this. After a suitable discussion, read the following quote, also from Mr. Rumsfeld:

> But you know why they want to be part of NATO? They're worried about their neighbors. Now if we are going to end up [in a room] with multiple nuclear states in the former Soviet Union [and] have them in a framework that is NATO-like where they can talk to each other . . . their behavior will alter. There is no question but that what we need to do . . . is to deal with the kinds of problems that exist today and that will exist over the coming decade. And NATO is probably not the perfect instrument.

Show the SCIS Videotape "Europe After the Cold War," Lesson 5, "European Security," to your class. Discuss with your class the idea that several of the Secretaries raise that NATO will have to change to remain relevant to post–Cold War Europe. In your discussion, also draw on the idea of the "Partnership for Peace" that President Clinton proposed to NATO and Eastern European states that wanted to join NATO during his January 1994 trip to Europe. (See the Study Guide for Lesson 5 for additional details.)

Divide students into seven groups, and distribute to each group one of the following problems/challenges facing Europe: ethnic rivalries, AIDS, immigration and refugees, the environment, terrorism, human rights, and nuclear threats. Have each group answer the following questions concerning its assigned problem:

1. What is the problem and how is it affecting Europe?
2. Can this problem be considered a security threat to Europe? Why?
3. What type of organization could best solve this problem? Describe it.
4. Could one of the existing security organizations in Europe (NATO, the WEU, CSCE) solve the problem? If not, could one of these organizations be restructured to solve the problem?
5. Should the United States be involved in security issues facing Europe? Should the U.S. be a member of security organizations that operate in Europe? Explain your answers.

Allow time for each group to share its answers and analysis with the class.

LESSON 5

EUROPEAN SECURITY

Activity 3:

HOW DO THE FORMER SECRETARIES FEEL ABOUT THE CHANGING ROLE OF NATO?

ACTIVITY OBJECTIVE

The student will be able to understand different perspectives about NATO's changing role in Europe.

MATERIALS AND RESOURCES

❑ SCIS Videotape "Europe After the Cold War," Lesson 5, "European Security"

❑ Index cards or blank paper

STRATEGIES

Remind students that many people currently question the role of NATO and other security organizations in Europe. Tell them that they are going to hear from some former Secretaries of State and Secretaries of Defense about how they feel about the changing role of NATO.

Divide the class into 10 small groups. Write each of the following names on an index card and give one card to each group: Edmund Muskie, Dean Rusk, Cyrus Vance, Henry Kissinger, William Rogers, Alexander Haig, George Shultz, Donald Rumsfeld, James Schlesinger, Frank Carlucci. Show the SCIS Videotape "Europe After the Cold War," Lesson 5, "European Security."

Have students watch the videotape and study the biographies of the former Secretaries, found in the front of Europe After the Cold War, to determine how their assigned secretary views the changing role of NATO. (Students may use the transcript of the tape for additional information.)

After students have viewed the tape, allow each group time to determine whether the secretary is liberal (prefers a change), conservative (does not favor any type of change) or moderate (somewhere in between) on this issue. Call on one student from each group to represent the views of the secretary. Tape the name of the former secretary on them so the class can determine whom they represent. Have the group stand up and form a horseshoe at the front of the classroom. They should stand according to the secretary's opinion of the need to change the NATO. (For example, Donald Rumsfeld believes it should be changed, so he is liberal on this issue and should stand on the left. Alexander Haig believes NATO must stay for security purposes; he would stand on the right of the horseshoe.) Let each student representing a secretary defend his/her place to stand on the horseshoe. Remind students that a person can be liberal on one issue and conservative on another.

Next have each student in the class come and stand in the horseshoe (you may need to re-arrange the desks) according to his or her own opinion about the future role of NATO.

Call on students at random to defend their own placement. Finally, have students stand according to their beliefs about the role the United States should play in the security problems of Europe.

Secretaries of Defense: Clockwise: David Gergen (moderator), Donald Rumsfeld, James Schlesinger, Elliot Richardson, Robert McNamara, and Caspar Weinberger

Secretaries of State: Clockwise: William Rogers, Alexander Haig, George Shultz, Dean Rusk, Henry Kissinger, Edmund Muskie, and Edwin Newman (moderator)

World Leaders Conference I: From left: Former Prime Minister of the United Kingdom James Callaghan, Former Chancellor of the Federal Republic of Germany Helmut Schmidt and Former Prime Minister of Japan Yasuhiro Nakasone

TRANSCRIPTS

BACKGROUND LESSON: The Cold War in Europe
"U.S. Soviet Relations: Demobilization to Detente," *The Dean Rusk Tapes – 1985*

LESSON 1: The Fall of Eastern European Communism
The Fourth Annual Report of the Secretaries of Defense – November 30, 1990
The Fifth Annual Report of the Secretaries of State – December 13, 1991

LESSON 2: The European Union
The Fifth Annual Report of the Secretaries of Defense – December 13, 1991
The Tenth Annual Report of the Secretaries of State – January 8, 1993

LESSON 3: Nationalism in Europe
The Tenth Annual Report of the Secretaries of State – January 8, 1993

LESSON 4: The German Question
The Seventh Annual Report of the Secretaries of State – October 27, 1989
The Eighth Annual Report of the Secretaries of State – October 12, 1990
The Tenth Annual Report of the Secretaries of State – January 8, 1993
The First Annual Berlin Conference of World Leaders – March 5, 1992

LESSON 5: European Security
The Sixth Annual Report of the Secretaries of State – December 9, 1988
The Eighth Annual Report of the Secretaries of State – October 12, 1990
The Sixth Annual Report of the Secretaries of Defense –December 4, 1992

TRANSCRIPT FOR BACKGROUND LESSON
THE DEAN RUSK TAPES - 1985

EDWIN NEWMAN   Mr. Rusk, during the Second World War, the United States and the Soviet Union were allies, perhaps more out of necessity than desire. Nevertheless, they were allies. Soon after the war, the world divided into two armed camps. How did this come about and why?

DEAN RUSK   At the end of the war, we ran into some problems. We and they had rather different views about how defeated Germany should be handled. We thought they were very late getting into the war against Japan; they made only a minor contribution to that end of the war. Things got off to a rather poor start. Most of us remember from our history or direct experience the sad story of the 1930s, when my generation of students was led down the path into the catastrophe of a World War II which could have been prevented. But most people have forgotten just what happened just after VJ-Day. We demobilized almost completely and almost overnight. By the summer of 1946 we did not have a single division in our army nor a single group in our air force that could be considered ready for combat. The ships of our navy were being put into mothballs as fast as we could find berths for them. Those that remained afloat were being manned by skeleton crews. Believe it or not, for three fiscal years, '47, '48, and '49, our defense budget came down to a little over $11 billion a year, groping for a target of $10 billion. We were disarmed. So were Britain and France. In one of the wartime conferences, Churchill mentioned to Mr. Stalin the views of the Pope on a particular point. Apparently Mr. Stalin said, "The Pope? How many divisions does he have?" He looked out across the West and he saw the divisions melting away. So what did he try to do? He tried to keep the northwest province of Iran, the first case before the UN Security Council. He demanded two eastern provinces of Turkey — Aurs and Cartahan. He supported the guerrillas going after Greece, using bases in places like Albania and Yugoslavia and Bulgaria. He brushed aside the wartime agreements which might have given the peoples of Eastern Europe some say in their political future, he had a hand in the communist coup d'etat in Czechoslovakia, he blockaded Berlin, and he gave the green light to the North Koreans to go after South Korea. Those were the events that started the Cold War.

EDWIN NEWMAN   And you think that the United States demobilization had a direct connection with this?

DEAN RUSK   Oh yes. I think that, in effect, we subjected Joseph Stalin to intolerable temptations. In the early thirties I was living near Potsdam, and I had a little canoe on the lakes there. One day I pulled the canoe up on a little beach and went into a restaurant to have lunch. When I came out, my canoe was gone. I notified the water police, and about an hour later they came puttering up in a motor boat, towing my canoe. They said, "Here is your canoe. We have the thief and he will be punished, but we're fining you five marks for tempting thieves." I had not locked my canoe. I think we tempted thieves by this extraordinary demobilization just after World War II. It was not until 1950 that we began to build up our armed forces in any significant way. Some politicians, the media, and public opinion have tended to swing like a pendulum, back and forth, between something called detente and the Cold War as though it were "either/or." In fact, both elements have been involved in our relationship with the Soviet Union throughout this post-war period. We and the

Soviets share a fundamental common interest, and that is the prevention of all-out nuclear war. No one in his right mind, either in Washington or in Moscow, would deny that. If we can find points of agreement on other matters, large or small, which can help to broaden that base of common interest and reduce the range of issues over which violence might occur, the effort has to be made.

This search for agreement did not begin in the early seventies when President Nixon and Mr. Kissinger talked so much about detente. It started right after World War II. We and the British and the Canadians took into the United Nations a plan called the Baruch Plan under which all fissionable materials would be turned over to the United Nations to be used solely for peaceful purposes. There would be no nuclear weapons in the hands of any nation, including ourselves. Unfortunately, we could not get serious discussions with the Soviet Union on that plan. There was one of those fleeting moments in history where an opportunity got away. Shortly after that, President Truman invited the Russians to participate in the Marshall Plan. It was the Soviets who walked out of that Paris meeting of European governments, to put their heads together and frame a reply to this invitation. When they walked out they dragged a very reluctant Czechoslovakia and Poland along with them.

Then during the Eisenhower period we achieved the Austrian State Treaty which removed all occupying forces from Austria, allowing that fine little country to go into the future as independent and neutral. It took hundreds of negotiations to accomplish that. It was a brilliant piece of preventive diplomacy. Moving into the Kennedy and Johnson years, we began that decade with two very serious crises: the crisis over Berlin in '61-62 and the crisis over Cuban missiles. Despite those crises, President Kennedy and his senior colleagues felt that it was just too late in history for two nuclear superpowers to pursue a policy of total hostility across the board.

Despite those crises of the early sixties we've set in motion things that produced the Nuclear Test Ban Treaty in 1963, the Civil Air Agreement for flights between New York and Moscow, a Consular Agreement which helped us to give somewhat better protection to Americans traveling in the Soviet Union, two important space treaties, the Treaty on the Non-Proliferation of Nuclear Weapons, and negotiations which eventuated in the Anti-Ballistic Missile Treaty in the early Nixon years. That was continued during the Nixon period with a new agreement on Berlin, the recognition, of the two Germanys of each other, and their joint membership in the United Nations, reducing greatly the prospect that Berlin would once again become a focus of crisis among the great powers. As far as I can see into the future, the Russians are not likely to trust us, and we're not likely to trust them. But you can have workable agreements between those who do not trust each other if you can verify or ascertain performance on the agreements.

TRANSCRIPT FOR LESSON ONE

DAVID GERGEN   Eastern Europe is now experiencing some greater difficulties with its democracies. What security challenges do these changes pose for the United States? How should we respond?

JAMES SCHLESINGER   Well I think the first point to be made is that six months ago our focus was on Eastern Europe and the liberation of the former satellites that had shaken off Soviet rule. We hoped that these countries would emerge into democracies — that they would achieve economic reform permitting them to sustain a rising standard of living, and that they would become part of Europe, part of the free world. They have been hit very hard by the developments in the Gulf. In the first place, the Soviets announced that they were going to require hard currency from the former satellites for oil and then the oil price for them more than doubled. And as a result, their prospects for economic improvement have deteriorated badly. Their internal politics have deteriorated as well. Disenchantment is spreading.

ROBERT MCNAMARA   I think we should recognize that no state has ever transitioned from an autocratic political structure in a centrally planned economy toward, not to, but toward, a pluralistic democratic structure in a market influenced economy. That has never been done. No human being knows how to do it in an orderly fashion. It is not going to happen in an orderly fashion. China has made progress, but it erupted in Tianamen Square. Poland was making progress, and it has led to [a] very divisive election. The Soviet Union is making progress [but] it's on the verge of disintegration. This is what we have to expect. There is going to be instability in Eastern and Central Europe and in the Soviet Union for years, and I'm afraid decades ahead. Does that present a great security challenge? There are security challenge elements of it. We must be very careful to deal with those. I think we can. Much more difficult will be dealing with the political, economic and social challenges. And the first proposition I'd put to you, is we must be tolerant. It is not going to happen quickly. It's not going to happen in an orderly fashion. We must not say, "Well, to hell with them. They've made all these mistakes and therefore we're not going to release our controls on export and technology, we're not going to give them most favorite nation trade status, and we're not going to provide the economic and technical assistance that they need that's within our power to give." So, I urge that we make every possible effort to assist them economically, technically, and in terms of political relationships that are still a major factor adversely affecting them. Now, I don't suggest that that takes a lot of money. We don't want to pour money down a rat hole, and we will be pouring money down a rat hole if we just ship over huge quantities of it to pour into a society that has no sound economic plan for utilizing those funds.

DONALD RUMSFELD   The reality is, [that] when a totalitarian system crumbles and the control over people eases, the bad people as well as the good people, become free. And there is no question but that the pressures for nationalistic aspirations — the anti-Semites, the fascists, there's all kinds of people who suddenly have much freer reign — it is going to be untidy. I worry a little bit about it when we — and I think that Bob made a good point — try to distinguish between money assistance and other kinds of assistance. I think there is always a risk in a situation like this that we will rush in with money — other countries [like] the United States — and do more harm than good. When you start sending food to Poland — the one piece there that might have been working is the agricultural side — you end up creating disincentives for people to buy seed, plant it, buy horses and tractors or whatever they need to grow food. And we end up disrupting, and we have to be very careful. I think one of the most important things we can do is insist that whatever we do, we want each of those countries to permit the free flow of people across their borders, because to the extent there's unemployment in those countries and those people leave, it's an enormous benefit. First of all, there are fewer unemployed that need to be fed. Second, they're earning hard currency in some other country — the United States or Western Europe. Third, they're developing a work ethic, and skills and knowledge doing some work there. And when they go, they're learning a language. They send hard currency back. There's no question but that there's that movement.

SOD V-1991

DAVID GERGEN   Secretary Schlesinger, you've written that you believe Eastern Europe should be at the highest priority for United States foreign policy, defense policy. Could you elaborate on that a moment?

JAMES SCHLESINGER   The United States, it seems to me, has both moral and political obligations in the region. For forty-five years we have said, once you throw off the shackles of the Soviet Union, you can count on us. We will be there. In 1989–1990, those shackles were thrown off, and what happened? We sent them a book of advice on how to adapt to the free market. The fact of the matter is that their economies are in shambles and living standards will decline without outside assistance, and without hope. As living standards decline, disenchantment will set in and we will have ugly governments in Eastern Europe. Poland is in trouble already. Czechoslovakia, for different reasons, is in trouble because of disunity. Only at this moment does Hungary seem to be able to make the adjustment from the command economy to the market economy. They deserve our help.

DAVID GERGEN   Therefore, you would increase American assistance?

JAMES SCHLESINGER   I would indeed. I would contrast American performance after 1945, the Marshall plan. It took us two years, by the way, to recognize the problems of Eastern Europe. And it was only after that cold winter of 1947 that we responded to Western Europe. Once again, two years have gone by. But, there is still time to preserve these countries for democratic systems, and to gradually, over the course of several decades [and] with the support of Western Europe, integrate them into the larger family of democratic nations.

ELLIOT RICHARDSON   There's a difference though, Jim, between the situation of Eastern Europe now and the situation of Western Europe in the immediate aftermath of World War II. In the case of the latter, they'd been through the destructive war, but they had free market economies up to and through the war. And so they needed help to rebuild to get going again. The problem with Eastern Europe is that they do not have the basic infrastructure of a working competitive economy. And the problem, as Bob touched on a while back, is that you can very easily allocate resources to that kind of situation to no real constructive, long-term purpose. And the question of how to use aid in that context is a very difficult problem.

JAMES SCHLESINGER   It is indeed a difficult problem [and] it is a more demanding problem for the reason that you point out. But that points to the need for technical assistance — people who can teach them how a market works, what double entry bookkeeping is, [etc.]

ELLIOT RICHARDSON   I thought you were speaking pejoratively about the proposition that that's all we were doing.

JAMES SCHLESINGER   There is also the problem of the devastation that the collapse of the communist economic system has brought. All of their capital is destroyed as if it had been destroyed by war. And we have not recognized that as yet.

DAVID GERGEN   A brief rejoinder by Don Rumsfeld.

DONALD RUMSFELD   Well, it seems to me that we're working around it, but there is no question but that their future depends on the extent to which, with help, they are capable and able of creating an environment that's hospitable to investment and savings. Until that happens in those countries, money will flee rather than go in, and, as Bob suggested, what does go in won't help. Not only in some instances won't it help, it'll hurt to the extent [that when] you have the beginnings of a viable agricultural situation and you have people risking investment — growing things, distributing it — and you rush in with a bucket of food, you destroy that incentive for them to be doing what they are doing. We have to be extremely careful how we help them.

DAVID GERGEN   But would you rush in with more technical assistance? I think that was the point Secretary Schlesinger was making.

DONALD RUMSFELD   I think that technical assistance is enormously valuable. I think they need more than technical assistance [and] one of the ways they will get it is by creating the right kind of an environment so investment's willing to go in.

JAMES SCHLESINGER   And by the way, our European partners better do something. We keep saying trade not aid. And the East Europeans are permitted to trade freely except for those commodities that are actually marketable — like agricultural commodities, steel and textiles. All of their industrial products that can't withstand Western competition can flow into the common market easily. If we say that they must rely upon the market place, we have to allow their marketable commodities to come in. The West Europeans have been quite unreceptive to that notion.

TRANSCRIPT FOR LESSON TWO

DAVID GERGEN   Secretary Weinberger, the United States' position publicly is that we support and welcome a strong, integrated Europe. In private, some are expressing reservations that a strong, integrated Europe may mean less of an American presence, the diminishment of NATO, a decoupling in effect. What is your evaluation?

CASPAR WEINBERGER   Both publicly and privately I've expressed a lot of worries about the transformation of a true common market which I support, into a whole new country with the diminished or eliminated sovereignty of all the historic nations that make up the European community. I think it's very much against our interests to do this — to support measures that would actually encourage the creation of a separate European defense force excluding the United States. I think that the goal of the Soviet Union all through the seventies and eighties was to decouple the United States from Europe. I think it would be very ironic, very unhappy and very unfortunate if that goal succeeded as the Soviet Union is crumbling into ashes. I think it's vital for the United States to stay coupled to Europe, and it's vital for us to continue to strengthen and support NATO — the most successful alliance in the world's history [that] has kept the peace for well over forty years. I think that all of this talk of a totally separate sovereign Europe with France, Germany and Britain being told from Brussels how much they can have in their budgets for various items and that they can't do anything they want within their own territories, which is starting to happen right now is not in our interests. Britain was told a few days ago that they couldn't build two roads or a bridge that they wanted to build. I don't think we should stand passively by and say this is fine. A common market, yes, that is in our interest, very much so, but I don't think an integrated sovereign Europe that destroys the sovereignty of all the historic states that have been allied with us, [and] with whom we have excellent relationships, is in our interests.

DAVID GERGEN   They seem to be proceeding independently without much regard for . . .

CASPAR WEINBERGER   Well, I think they are proceeding on the assumption that we don't care, that it doesn't make any difference to us, and that there is no fear, that anything they would do will not alienate or harm the ultimate support which they know they will need from the United States. I think we should exert our influence and make some of the points that I've just tried to make so that they will know that there is a definite cost to tossing aside NATO and to substituting for it some kind of a Franco-German brigade, or something of that kind, in the hope that that can keep the peace in Europe. I don't think that if Europe falls, America can stand very long. And I consequently think that we should stay aligned with Europe, not as an altruistic thing, but in our own interest as we've done all these years in NATO. I'm very much afraid that this attempt to turn a common market into a whole new country is something that is very much against our interests.

DAVID GERGEN   Bob McNamara.

ROBERT MCNAMARA   Two points. First, the structure of Europe and the relationship among the European nations is for the Europeans to decide. [Even] if we wanted to, we couldn't influence it very much. Secondly, I strongly agree with both Cap and Don that it's in our interests and theirs that we remain. They used the word "coupled" and I think that's a perfectly reasonable word. But what I see is two balls of relatively equal weight — economically, militarily, [and] politically joined by a bar of common interest. We've got to maintain that bar of common interest. One action that is required to maintain it, is for the Europeans to make clear that they will involve themselves in what are called "out of area responsibilities." And I see Don and Cap nodding their heads. This is a very important point. It is unresolved today. It means either NATO must change their policies and agree, let's say to help in the Gulf, or alternatively there must be a Western European union or some other force that will be integrated with ours in actions of common purpose and common goals.

SOS X-1993

EDWIN NEWMAN   We have seen the move toward a united Europe break down. Is this something that is troubling to the United States?

GEORGE SHULTZ   It hasn't broken down, it just hasn't gone ahead as far as perhaps people hoped it might two or three years ago. There's been a big set of intervening events. Now the question is, and it comes right back again to this refugee and immigration problem, to what degree should Europe, the European community as they say, deepen itself, and to what degree should it try to reach out more to these newly free states and bring them in. They've got to have the immigration problem on their minds for just the reasons Bill said. The better it can be in those countries, the less of a problem there is.

WILLIAM ROGERS   Another point in that connection should be made. At the time the European Community was trying to consolidate, [there was] the problem of unification of Germany, which made it very difficult because the Germans had to assimilate all the East Germans into their nation. As George indicated, we have to hope that Europe is unified. I think it'll take longer than they expected. They already have eliminated a lot of their customs barriers and they have eliminated some of their immigration barriers. But that's going to be a problem. I think it's going to take them a long time to have monetary union, I think.

ALEXANDER HAIG   I agree with this. Maastricht was just too ambitious, too impatient, [and] tried to achieve too much. And it was a hiccup. Now the momentum is continuing more slowly towards additional integration. George raised a very important question. Is it going to be exclusive, or is it going to be hospitable and outreaching? I think Maastricht at least, was encouraging from the standpoint that they want to reach out to the free trade area of Northern Europe, to Eastern Europe, and perhaps even to the republics of the Soviet Union. And I think this is the kind of Europe we want to see.

EDMUND MUSKIE   Well, the interesting thing about Maastricht, in addition to what Al has had to say, is that Maastricht was targeted and scheduled way ahead of the event, and a lot of the things that had to flow from unity, had to be a yielding up of national identity from the point of view of those [members]. Maastricht meant that your European currency, which did not yet have a value or an identity or that they were willing to accept in return for their bank accounts in their own national currency, was going to be abandoned.   The business of free travel has gone very well.

We've all been traveling around and we see how freely the Europeans now travel without any kind of border problems at all. It's very easy. But giving up your currency, that's a little more difficult. And as the world grows, and as inflation [and] all the rest of it grows, the smaller economic units which are represented by many countries who are members of the United Nations and of Europe, begin to see their identity and security slipping. Part of this is psychological, but I understand it. I've already made it clear [that] I'm opposed on this program. I think the Polish people, if they were to be included here, would be very reluctant to give up zloty. So currency seems to be the Maastricht element that really disturbs as a symbol of other things.

ALEXANDER HAIG   Let me make an observation about immigration because, as Bill pointed out, it is a very critical problem. The roots of that problem are more economic today than they are political. Our problem is a world in which we have "haves" and "have nots" and the disparity between the two is insurmountable. And that's why we are faced with this. So what we are really dealing with is a macro-economic problem in the long term. And that is how to get a better distribution of the benefits of modernization to the world at large. And that's a major chore for us for decades to come.

TRANSCRIPT FOR LESSON THREE

EDWIN NEWMAN   We see Yugoslavia breaking up in the most horrible way. We see Czechoslovakia breaking up peacefully so far. But ethnic consciousness, I guess it can be called, seems to be everywhere and to be used as a basis for nationhood. Should the United States support nationalist movements where citizenship and political rights are based on ethnic identity or religious identity?

WILLIAM ROGERS   Well, I think it's a question of each one of these cases taken separately. In the case of Czechoslovakia, for example, what could the United States do to prevent that? The Czechs and Slovaks wanted to separate, they have separated, and they are two nations now. So we're going to have to deal with them. As far as Yugoslavia is concerned, that of course presents another problem. The real question is do we get involved militarily. My own view is I don't think we should now. I think we may have to eventually, but I don't think we should at the moment. I think that we have a representative — Cy Vance is over there — of the European community, and they recommend that we do not engage militarily at the moment.

ALEXANDER HAIG   We must be advocates of rule of law and peaceful change and due process. And if in the process of bringing ethnic purity to the fore there is violation of law, we must oppose it. If it happens through peaceful means and negotiation, then we can endorse it.

EDWIN NEWMAN   Are you suggesting that we should become militarily involved?

ALEXANDER HAIG   In this instance there is violation of law on the part of the Serbian leaders, and as a world community we must move to oppose it. What I'm saying is unilateral American involvement would be a disaster.

EDWIN NEWMAN   I just want to shift, if I may, to another point. In August of 1990, Iraq invaded Kuwait, seven months...

GEORGE SHULTZ   Are you going to shift away from this without giving me a crack at the subject?   (LAUGHTER.)

EDWIN NEWMAN   How could I consider doing such a thing?

WILLIAM ROGERS   You had your choice at first, [but] you interrupted Ed.
(LAUGHTER.)

EDWIN NEWMAN   Well, please go ahead sir.

GEORGE SHULTZ   Well, I don't know why I'm smiling because what is going on over there in Bosnia is horrible by any standard. There is no way, I think, that you can stand around and say mediate when an agreement is announced and at the same time Sarajevo is being shelled. And we have incontrovertible evidence of all sorts of violations of people, of systematic rape of young girls, of all sorts of terrible things. We have a situation where all of the arms are in the hands of one party and none in the other. So, we have an embargo that tells the forces that might want to defend themselves — that do want to defend themselves — that they can't get any arms. I saw a man who was a world-class soccer player going back to his home, and [I] asked why he did that. He said, "A man who won't defend his home doesn't deserve to have one."

EDWIN NEWMAN   So he went back to Yugoslavia?

GEORGE SHULTZ   He went back. And when I was in office we called a guy like that a freedom fighter and we supported him. And I think we should support him.

EDWIN NEWMAN   How far do you think the United States should go militarily then?

GEORGE SHULTZ   I agree with Al that we should get other people to go with us. And the United Nations has already stated a "no fly zone." NATO has said that it's ready to be involved. Whether in the clutch or not it remains to be seen, but all of those things are there. We have gone to the United Nations and pointed up these human rights matters which are terrible. We now in retrospect say, "the Holocaust, how terrible that was." And how just as terrible it was that somehow it happened and nobody paid any attention. Nobody did anything about it. Well, we have exactly the same thing. What is ethnic cleansing? We have exactly the same thing right in front of us, and what are we doing? Are we just going to sit around and say it's terrible?

ALEXANDER HAIG   The profound lesson here, George, is that when we were confronted in the Gulf, the United States established the consensus in the United Nations, it established the consensus through leadership in the Arab League. We failed to do so in Yugoslavia. And this underlies very, very importantly the initial discussion we had. The Americans must continue to lead.

WILLIAM ROGERS   I don't know what we'd do if we got in Yugoslavia. Shoot down a few airplanes? That's a start. But where do you stop when that continues? I mean, we still have in the United Nations, in Korea, 35,000 troops.

ALEXANDER HAIG   Thank God.

WILLIAM ROGERS   Well, do we want to take over? Once we shoot down a few airplanes and that doesn't work, what's the next step?

GEORGE SHULTZ   I'll give you some examples. We can allow people who want to fight to defend their own homes to get the armaments to do so. That's one thing we can do. Another thing we can do is to deny the tremendous advantages, I guess General Haig would agree to this, that comes to somebody who can fly low-level aircraft and helicopters over an area without anybody doing anything about it. So you get rid of that. We can do that. And third, we have the ability to take out military installations and things of that kind that just are a good shot across the bow. I think you get people's attention that way. There's no doubt about it.

WILLIAM ROGERS   You get their attention, no doubt about that, but are you going to have American boys killed there? They've been fighting in that part of the world forever, and they still have these terrible battles among themselves. Whether we're going to be able to solve that by military means or not is very doubtful in my

162

mind. We've never been able to before. And every time we got involved in one of these — unless it's in the Gulf where we had a definite objective. We stated the objective, [and] we used a lot of military forces.

ALEXANDER HAIG   Oh, Bill, come on. I remember the debate before our entry into the Gulf. My God, there were 200,000 American casualties — a quagmire from which we would never be able to withdraw. Anyone who's against doing anything and would rather negotiate any problem is going to take that line.

WILLIAM ROGERS   The only thing I object to is actually the use of military force. Now, if we decide that we want to shoot down airplanes, and as Al said, we get the United Nations and other nations to do that, I think maybe we'll have to do it. But I don't think we should do it now.

GEORGE SHULTZ   I'd like to emphasize a different point that's related, however. To me, about the most difficult problem of governance around the world — not just in Yugoslavia, not just in the old Soviet Union, but say, look across at India, [and] look at little places like Sri Lanka — is how you govern over diversity of various kinds. You identified some of the elements of diversity. And to some extent you can allow people to divide themselves. But, nevertheless, in the kind of world that Al described, that we all know is there, that Ed described, everything is brought together. There are lots of places, the United States being the outstanding example, where there is inherent diversity. You can't get away from it. And so you have to learn how to govern over it — how to so arrange things that people can honor their varying roots, but at the same time have an overall common purpose that allows them to live together successfully. And one of the tragedies in the old Yugoslavia is that Sarajevo was exactly a little showcase of people of different backgrounds living together successfully and that showcase has been destroyed in this process.

EDWIN NEWMAN   Well, I almost think from what Secretary Rogers said earlier that he thought it probably was hopeless to expect these people to live together peacefully.

WILLIAM ROGERS   There are civil wars going on all over — among ethnic groups, among tribal groups in Africa. And the idea that somehow we can make those people, by force or coercion, accept our principles, I think is misleading. I think we should try. I think we should take a moral position, and that's what our nation has done over the years and I think the new administration will continue to do that. I just think that the use of force to try to — I'm talking about military force now — make other people do what we think they should do is fruitless and dangerous.

ALEXANDER HAIG   Well, that's a happy generalization with which I fully concur.

WILLIAM ROGERS   Good.

ALEXANDER HAIG   On the other hand, I think we have in this world, and this is an important issue, Ed, a transparency that's come out of globalism, which now makes it impossible for heads of state and government to ignore atrocities, injustices, and conflict around the world. That's what happened in Somalia. My God, the people of Sudan starved wholesale, and nobody said anything until the American television and press got on it and you saw it every night. People demanded action. The same thing is going to occur in Yugoslavia.

TRANSCRIPT FOR LESSON FOUR

HEDRICK SMITH   I'd like to go back to the German question, which has come up a couple of times. I think it's hard for Americans sitting here to realize how fast things are moving in Central Europe — the developments in East Germany, the sentiment, as you've suggested, Dr. Kissinger, in East Germany for eventual reunification, the raising of that issue again but in West Germany. What I seem to hear around this table are two quite different views. I think you're suggesting that the reunification of Germany is inevitable and we better begin to factor that into our long-term thinking. And if I hear correctly, both Secretary Rusk and Secretary Haig are suggesting that the reunification of Germany would be an enormously dangerous thing...question. Should the United States be working with Britain, France and others, and West Germany to prevent this?

ALEXANDER HAIG   No. Let me address that. First, I would add to Henry's already made observation that this is historically, probably inevitable. But it's also very important in the near term that the United States or other Western powers not be perceived by the German people to be opposed to the ultimate goal of reunification. That would be very dangerous and counterproductive.

HEDRICK SMITH   You're talking reunification within the Western Alliance? And would the Soviets accept that?

ALEXANDER HAIG   Well now, the German government itself, the Bonn government, has already laid out its perception of unity very clearly. They don't use the term reunification. They talk about a unified Germany under a confederation or a federation of states. This would be an elaboration of their current lander system in the West, but [it] would put East Germany into a sort of confederation with Bonn but not require changes in system or changes in fundamental approaches and outlooks. That's the West German government's position today. I think we have to help them in knowing that there must be conditions for reunification which do not create the specters of danger that Henry's talked about, or the possibility of a Europe [being] paranoid about a reunified Germany. The French are already concerned.

HEDRICK SMITH   Is this a Germany united with the West? And if so, will the Russians buy it? Or is this a neutral Germany? And if so, will the West buy it?

ALEXANDER HAIG   Slow and evolutionary. And as Cy has correctly pointed out, we can't drive them in the East into paranoia either.

EDWIN NEWMAN   Are you worried about the prospect of German domination of Europe?

CYRUS VANCE   No. I don't think there's any question but that Germany will increase in its economic strength. It will end up, in my judgement, being the dominant economic power in the European community and in the expanded and integrated European community that is coming along. I think that this should not be frightening to us. I think that we have the capability to strengthen our economy. I think we are taking some steps along that road now, and that we should be able to compete with the new integrated European community, and to be able to compete with Germany. So, I don't find that frightening.

SOS X-1993

EDWIN NEWMAN Is Germany a country to worry about?

EDMUND MUSKIE There is a problem because there is a point of view in the world that we cannot forget what Germany was responsible for decades ago. Whether that's justified or not is for Germany to demonstrate in one way or another. I don't think that follows — that the Germany of Hitler, you know, will become the Germany of tomorrow. Not at all.

ALEXANDER HAIG Let me express a thread of optimism. Germany has lived for forty years with democracy. It is now imbedded in the culture and the heart and soul of every German I know. What you're witnessing on the fringes is going to spend its course.

GEORGE SHULTZ In many ways, the most impressive thing about these problems that have been so publicized in Germany recently, is the way the Germans themselves are reacting to them. You have outpourings into the streets of the German people saying, "No, we don't want that kind of extremism." So I think that's a pretty impressive reaction.

WILLIAM ROGERS One of the reasons that they're having difficulty in Germany is because of the flow of immigrants. And if the European community continues with no restrictions on immigration, this problem is going to recur, not only in Germany, but other places.

EDWIN NEWMAN What is going to happen then, if the fighting goes on in various parts of what used to be the Soviet Union, for example? Will there be a flood of refugees coming?

WILLIAM ROGERS Sure. Absolutely. Every nation that is really down in the dumps and having a lot of problems wants to move somewhere else. And the normal place to move to is the countries that are successful.

WORLD LEADERS-1992

MARVIN KALB So I gather you would not share the view that Germany at this particular point will emerge as the superpower within Europe, bullying its way toward a series of nationalistic ends, but would submerge itself into the greater interest of a united Europe.

HELMUT SCHMIDT I do not foresee, over the rest of this century, that Germany will develop into a financial superpower. It might in the next century. I would rather hope that the European community as a whole does develop into a superpower, a financial economic superpower — into one entity, rather than the mass of nation states inside the community. This hinges very much on the problem of whether we muster the guts to give up on our national currencies and central bank systems, or whether we maintain our national currencies. If deutsche marks and francs and sterling are being maintained as national currencies, in that case, certainly Germany will become the outstanding, "sticking out," financial superpower in the beginning of the next century.

JAMES CALLAGHAN   This raises a most serious problem as a matter of fact. I think that the German leadership has been extremely wise since the end of the war. Nevertheless, we have to face this fact, and the Germans will have to face this fact. Indeed, I know it's well known to many of you already. There is an apprehension in the rest of Europe that Germany with 80 million people, with its economic strength, with its dedication, its self-discipline, will be such an overwhelming weight in the community that the rest of Europe is for the most part worried that if it throws in its lot into this community with one currency, which will be the German mark — let there be no doubt about that — that Germany could then carry us down roads that the rest of us would not wish to go. How we overcome this, I do not know. It is a real fear. Germany, I think, has done all she could to insure that these apprehensions are stilled. But history, as well as your economic strength, insures that they are still present.

MARVIN KALB   Do you feel that if Britain were — as I said earlier in the program — now to place its strategic heart in Europe, fully, unreservedly, that it could serve as a kind of balance against the emergence of a Germany that would produce apprehension?

JAMES CALLAGHAN   What I think we are worried about is that if we have a common currency, if we have a common economic policy, the center will be Berlin or Bonn or wherever; it certainly will be in the heart of Germany. The periphery of which Britain will be one part as well as Scotland, Wales and the rest of it, will, because the industrial magnet will be based here, leave our people unemployed as soon as we have a common currency. Now, I'm not saying that this should necessarily determine it, but it is a very powerful factor if you go to the electorate and say, "Look here, we want to ditch sterling, hand it over to the mark and the Bundesbank." That's the only basis on which the Bundesbank would ever agree. And so you can understand this natural reserve arising out of a long tradition and a long history. And we're not alone. Other countries in Europe will feel the same when it comes to the real test.

HELMUT SCHMIDT   As a footnote, could I just mention to you, Jim, you're talking about Germany as an economic giant. It's a misnomer, because Germany right now is in the course of changing from a formidable capital exporter into a capital importer. And this will be the case for, roughly speaking, a decade or so. We need some enormous amounts of capital for East Germany, formerly GDR. And we even need some capital for the Russians, or the former Soviets, in order to help them get their troops out of German soil. We don't, even given the fact that we are saving 13 or 14% of our privately disposable income on average, generate enough capital for ourselves.

TRANSCRIPT FOR LESSON FIVE

EDWIN NEWMAN   Secretary Muskie, let's talk a bit about NATO and the possible effects on NATO, on the Western Alliance, of Gorbachev's speech and Gorbachev's policies. NATO came into being because of what was thought to be a threat from the Soviet Union to Western Europe. Apparently many Europeans, and not only Europeans, believe that threat is a great deal less than it used to be. [It is] still less now, because of the reforms taking place inside the Soviet Union. Secretary Kissinger, Secretary Vance, you wrote an article well before Mr. Gorbachev's speech in which you said, "It is time for NATO to redefine its goals and rededicate itself to new missions." What redefinition of goals do you recommend, and what new missions do you propose for NATO? Would you go first, Secretary Vance?

CYRUS VANCE   Yes, I think we have to realize that there have been substantial changes since NATO was founded. At the time of the founding of NATO, we had a nuclear monopoly that no longer exists. As a result of that, there have been questions raised about our commitment to it. Secondly, there has been, I believe, no real change in our commitment to it. That ought to be said and underscored. But, there are questions that have been raised by some of the people in NATO. In addition to that, there has been a resurgence in the economy of Europe, and we see added to that, in 1992, when we may see an integrated Europe. These are rather profound changes, and I think they are going to require us to take a look at what kind of changes, structural and otherwise, have to be made in order to have the most appropriate force for these changed times. One of the things that one, I think, ought to look at is what Dean has talked about — What role for the European forces should there be and should it change their relationship to our forces. This is something that we have got to work out together. So we ought to be sitting down right now, and from here forward, talking about redefining. Are there security things that ought to be done? Now, in addition to that, there are things on the economic side that have to be looked at in connection with what is going on with the European Community. That isn't NATO, but it does interrelate with NATO and what our overall posture will be.

HENRY KISSINGER   Since Secretary Vance and I wrote the article together, it's not surprising that we agree. (LAUGHTER.) And, so I share his views. I would summarize the issue to be as follows: When NATO was formed, the United States was overwhelmingly powerful economically. It had a nuclear monopoly and there was a perception of a danger of an imminent Soviet invasion of Europe based on the North Korean invasion of South Korea. All these conditions have changed. The United States is still powerful, but no longer predominant. The nuclear monopoly has long since disappeared. There's now something like nuclear parity, and Europe has gained in economic strength and cohesion. Now that it is stronger, it is better for it to develop its own concept of defense and harmonize it with ours. We should have enough self-confidence to realize that for Europe it will always be better to have us on their side in fighting aggression, than to do it alone. And if they think they can do it alone, why should we object? But they won't think this. It will strengthen cooperation and it will make the burdens their own burdens rather than ours. We need some coherence in approaches to the Soviets so that it doesn't trigger a race to Moscow, [where] every country tries, for domestic reasons, to prove that they can get to Gorbachev better than the others and make it an issue of domestic politics. These are the challenges, but I think they can be met.

EDWIN NEWMAN   Secretary Rogers.

WILLIAM ROGERS   I didn't help write the article, so I guess I can disagree. (LAUGHTER.) I think we want to be very careful about tinkering with NATO at the moment. NATO . . . if you go back and look at what we've said at previous meetings of this kind, where we've all taken the position — which I think is very sound . . . has probably been the strongest stabilizing force that we've had in our foreign policy since World War II. I think one of the objectives of Gorbachev is attempting to use his speech and his new policies to undercut the Alliance, and to weaken NATO.

CYRUS VANCE   What Henry and I have been talking about is in no way going to weaken NATO, indeed it will make NATO a much better, stronger organization, adapted to these times and not times that are long past. With respect to the question that you put forth — is there anything which he is doing which could weaken . . .

EDWIN NEWMAN   [Is there] any way it could work out to the disadvantage of the United States?

CYRUS VANCE   To the disadvantage of NATO. If it should lead to a weakening of our resolve or commitment, which it will not, to support NATO and to be a full-fledged member of NATO, yes, then it could. I don't see that in what he's suggesting. Bill, I think, has a somewhat different view — that somehow the blandishments of what he is saying will lead us to that.

WILLIAM ROGERS   No, I didn't say that. I said it's a possibility. No, I don't think he attempted to do that in his speech.

SOS VIII-1990

EDWIN NEWMAN   Is it conceivable that Germany might want to take itself out of NATO?

CYRUS VANCE   I don't think so.

ALEXANDER HAIG   I would like to say that if we didn't have a NATO today, we would have to create it. The simple facts are that the most credible guarantee that there will not be a resurrection of the loose cannon on the deck of Central Europe, is the American military presence in Europe — the NATO alliance as the security framework for the future of a changing Europe. Now, obviously NATO's going to have to change. I think one of the most vexing and difficult questions we're going to face in the period ahead is not NATO's continued presence, or Germany's continued presence in NATO, but the continued presence of nuclear systems on West German soil. They are precluded from East German soil, and I think correctly. This could be a devastating question. If there is a nuclear-free zone set up in West Germany, then the Americans will lose the basis and the rationale for maintaining our forces in Europe, and I think the alliance will collapse.

DEAN RUSK   Is there not the possibility that an over-arching security treaty in Europe would come to make sense? — [already] including all the NATO countries and all the countries of Eastern Europe, bound together in a common security agreement? We've gone through the struggles of the Cold War where such an idea seems a little repulsive to some people, but surely we could transform the European continent into a war-free continent.

EDWIN NEWMAN   Would it be, as well, free of the presence of the United States military?

DEAN RUSK   No, the United States ought to be, and Canada ought to be a part of that overall agreement.

CYRUS VANCE   I think that the Europeans would certainly agree on that, most all of them would.

GEORGE SHULTZ   If you had such a treaty and you didn't have a NATO, as Al said, you need to invent it because you have to have some means of being sure the treaty is [kept].

DEAN RUSK   That's right. And within that over-arching treaty you could make arrangements for German limitations on its armed forces, [and] maybe a nuclear-free Germany.

EDWIN NEWMAN   Secretary Muskie, the last word on this subject, please.

EDMUND MUSKIE   Just two brief points: One, I think NATO will be important for a long time to come as a consultative institution on security matters. The second point I would make is again highlighted by our current crisis in the Middle East. Until that crisis came along, NATO was always regarded as having relevance only with respect to Europe — never with respect to security risks outside of Europe. Now for the first time, the NATO countries have created this coalition, or helped create this coalition with respect to the Middle East. So there are common security interests outside of NATO that might well be addressed by the future.

SOD VI-1992

DAVID GERGEN   For the past forty years, as we all understand, NATO has been a bulwark of security for America and Western Europe. Should it guarantee the security of Eastern Europe?

DONALD RUMSFELD   I met with a group of Russian military, first when they were Soviet Union military and then later when they were Russian military, over a period of three or four years now. One of the comments was, "We want to be a part of NATO." And of course the immediate reaction you have to that is, "Well that's a funny thing for them to be saying." But you know why they want to be a part of NATO? They're worried about their neighbors. Now, if you're going to end up with multiple nuclear states in the former Soviet Union, having them in a framework that is NATO-like, where they can talk to each other in front of the smaller countries and with the United States. I might add, with the countries in the world that can help them economically, in the room, their behavior will alter. There is no question but that what we need to do as a country is what this country did in the late 1940s. Try to fashion arrangements that will in fact deal with the kinds of problems that exist today and will exist over the coming decade. And NATO is probably not the perfect instrument.

JAMES SCHLESINGER   We have a dilemma. We don't want to give up NATO, which is our instrument, which is the American point of entry into the councils of Europe, [and] which provided us with American domination of military strategy. We don't want to give that up. And as a consequence, what we need are new instruments of the sort that Don referred to. But those are different instruments in which the United States will not be dominant. Therefore, we are faced with this dilemma. We keep insisting that NATO is the answer to the new problems that are emerging.

DAVID GERGEN   So you think we ought to have these new forms of organizations supplemental to NATO, but take care of some of these new issues that are emerging, such as the security of Eastern Europe?

FRANK CARLUCCI   But don't kid yourself that it's ever going to have the kind of capabilities of NATO. It's a talking forum. Clearly, we need NATO, or the Atlantic Alliance. I think Jim was saying that in a positive sense. But I think Jim would also agree that NATO needs to change. NATO needs to look at out-of-area activities, out-of-area missions. That is very different than underwriting the security guarantees for all of Eastern Europe and the former Soviet Union.

ELLIOT RICHARDSON   You're right, but NATO has never been willing to look out there.

FRANK CARLUCCI   Well, they're going to have to.

HAROLD BROWN   There is, in the Western European Union, [a] long-dormant military possibility for the European countries that can, if it's handled right, act both as the European pillar of NATO and also for the European countries to operate outside the NATO area when Europeans see their interests as different from that of the United States. [That] is often the case.